SOMEWHERE BETWEEN KC/MO AND EAST ST. LOU
An Anthology of Missouri Poets

Edited by Jason Ryberg with special guest
editor, Maryfrances Wagner, Missouri Poet
Laureate, 2021-2023

Spartan
Press

Spartan Press
Kansas City, MO
spartanpress.com

Spartan
Press

Copyright © Jason Ryberg, 2022
First Edition: 1 3 5 7 9 10 8 6 4 2
ISBN: 978-1-958182-32-1
LCCN: 2022951164

Author photos: Dan Wright, John Garton,
Sondra M. Seiler, David Joel, Mark Berndt
Cover and title page image: Jon Lee Grafton

Special thanks to the editors of these publications:

Rick Christiansen: "Pig Lung Soup" / *The Raven's Perch,* "Not a Hero" / *The Rye Whiskey Review,* "Into the Can (Haibun)" *MacQueen's Quinterly,* **James D'Agostino**: "Quantum Tantrum" / *Sprung Formal,* **Patricia Cleary Miller**: "Rice" / *Poets at Large,* "Chris Norman, Small Bagpipes" / *Rockhurst Review,* "Mother Won't Buy Polypropylene" / *Rockhurst Review, Can You Smell the Rain, Pushcart,* "Mother Won't Wear Walking Shoes" / *New Letters, Can You Smell the Rain?,* "As the Firefly Passes through Flame" / *Rockhurst Magazine,* "At that Moment" / *Pot Pourri,* **Jose Faus:** "For Francisco Alarcon" / *Poetry Bay,* **Tina Hacker:** "Listening to Southern Women," "Looking for Helen" / *Potpourri,* "Sheba," "Death of a Gucci Handbag" / *Kansas City Voices,* "Counting Peas" / *Cutting It,* "Hiding Places" / *Coal City Review,* "The Ninotchka Syndrome" / *Listening to Night Whistles,* "Where Are You, Merle Oberon" / *I-70 Review,* "Jim Crow Crayons" / *The Fib Review,* "An Angel Flowers" / *Quantum Fairy Tales,* **Linda Rodriguez**: "The Wild City" / *Cutthroat, a Journal of the Arts,* "No More (Sestina For Standing Rock)" / *Red Earth,* "What River Says," "Crow Mother," "The Things She Gave Me," "Ofrenda" /*Dark Sister* (Mammoth Publications, 2018), "Outside Your House At Midnight," Coyote," "Conversation With My Mother's Picture" / *Heart's Migration* (Tia Chucha Press, 2009), "Reading At Night" / *Skin Hunger* (Scapegoat Press, 2007), "Dreaming of My Late Mother-in-law's House" / *Heart's Migration* (Tia Chucha Press, 2009), **Jemshed Khan: "**Jesús de Honduras, 2020" "The Tame Swans of Waterbury," "First Ladies Speak," "Maryville High School, 1973" / *I-70 Review,* "Slowly They Go" / *Fifth Estate,* "The Colonised Mind," "Interrogator" / *Speech in an Age of Certainty,* "UK Winter, 1963" / *Coal City Review,* "Wingnuts" / *The Shining Years,* "Dad's Last ER Visit" / *The Strategic Poet,* **Poet T.L. Sanders: "**To My Dear Neighbor," "For Love," "Truth," "In Time," "We Cover the Cover"/ *KC Voices, kNew* (Flying Ketchup Press, 2019), **Jane Ellen Ibur:** "What Mary Said" / *Both Wings Flappin', Still Not Flyin'* (PenUltimate Press, 2014), "Augusta" / *Eads Bridge: A Literary Review, Webster Review,* "Stagecoach," "Mrs. Noah – Two Weeks Out" / *The Little Mrs./ Misses* (PenUltimate Press, 2017), "Shooting Stars" / *New Harvest* (Brodsky Library Press, 2005), "Lady Dainty" / *American Journal of Poetry* - Volume 3, "Hibiscus" / *Boulevard,* "A Hot Dog Kind Of Girl" / *Spitball Magazine,* #43

Table of Contents

Introduction by Maryfrances Wagner

Rick Christiansen

James D'Agostino

Tina Hacker

Linda Rodriguez

Jemshed Khan

Poet T.L. Sanders

Victoria Garton

Jane Ellen Ibur

Introduction

During my time as Missouri's 6th Poet Laureate, I have had two major goals. The first has been to put poetry into the hands and ears of Missourians who don't usually read poetry or go to poetry readings. My second has been to promote or highlight Missouri poets and publishers. Thanks to all of the poets (over 50) who have participated in some part of one of the projects, and thanks to Jason Ryberg of Spartan press and Ben Furnish of BkMk press for production.

As a result of Covid, I have not been able to have the usual Missouri Poet Laureate travel experience for public appearances. I've given readings, talks, and keynotes, taught workshops, judged contests, participated in book festivals, written poems, published a book, re-issued a new edition of *Red Silk,* been interviewed, and traveled around some parts of the state. I have done many events while sitting at my computer on Zoom, so I decided I wanted to create some projects that would help me fulfill my two primary goals and reach all regions of the state in a meaningful way.

The most significant thing I have learned so far as Poet Laureate is how many fine poets have lived or worked in Missouri for a large part of their lives. Through my projects, I have tried to represent all regions of the state, multiple styles, and diversity, but I know there are still many poets out there I don't know or was not able to contact to be involved in one of my projects. I know I haven't begun to represent all Missouri poets, but I'm not done yet, so there's more to come.

My first project was to create ten podcasts called The Literary State. Each of these is a ten to twenty-minute podcast with a Missouri poet. Poets answer two questions about the craft of poetry, give a writing prompt, and read two of their poems. The podcasts are available on Anchor, Spotify, and Apple, or those interested can google them and listen on their phones or computers. The goal is that people will listen to them in their car, while cooking dinner, sitting at a table with a pen in hand ready to write, or anywhere they usually listen to podcasts. I also hope that teachers and professors will share them with their students as the podcasts offer valuable information about writing.

My second major project was to create Tiny Books to highlight eighteen more Missouri poets. Each of these tiny books includes one poem. Each of those poets received a quantity of tiny books to distribute to people who do not usually read poetry—the grocer, waiter, doctor, dentist, mail deliverer, grass cutter, neighbor, etc. These tiny books have been incredibly popular, and I wish I had thousands more of them to distribute since there are over six million people in Missouri, and I wish everyone could have at least one of them. Some have reacted in wonderful ways of helping to spread them around for many to read, and I thank them for that.

The third project is this one—two anthologies. Ten poems from ten more Missouri poets in two anthologies published by Spartan press and in partnership with *I-70 Review*. Welcome to the words of ten Missouri poets in this anthology. Enjoy.

-Maryfrances Wagner, Missouri's 6th
Missouri Poet Laureate 2021-2023

SOMEWHERE
BETWEEN KC/MO AND
EAST ST.LOU

And the old folks were strumming that same old refrain
Way down in Missouri when I heard this lullaby
While the stars were blinking and the moon was shining high
And the old folks were humming the banjos were
    strumming so sweet and low

-Johnny Cash, *Missouri Waltz*

Rick Christiansen

Rick Christiansen is a former corporate executive, stand-up comedian, actor and director. His work is published or forthcoming in *Oddball Magazine, Muddy River Poetry Review, Stone Poetry Journal, The Raven's Perch, The Rye Whiskey Review, As It Ought to Be Magazine, WINK Magazine, MacQueen's Quinterly* and other journals, anthologies and magazines He is the co-host of SpoFest Poetry and Prose. And, along with Damian Ward Hey, he is editing the forthcoming *Dead Pets Poetry Anthology,*. He lives in Missouri near his eight grandchildren.

Advice from my Muse

We mold happiness like a new clay pot,
fashioned within the circle of our arms.
Joy must be manufactured.

We are survivors in this forest.
Like a fern living amongst the tree roots,
we make our peace with any soil.

I tell you to be as grateful as the circumstances of your
    life deserve.
I am the voice you have been given,
it is important that you let me sing of these things.

There is strength in acceptance.
Sometimes you must swallow without question.
Trust me to help you find your way.

I know it is easier to just be clever:
build a stackable life,
reside in a Universe of almost.

But each morning when you are fresh and still in
    your robe,
with your dog and your coffee beside you,
let me help you write what we know.

Pig Lung Soup

Everything must be chewed and digested

You remember
many times
In the back seat of a car
Holding your whole world
In a paper bag
In your lap

No idea where
You are going
Just knowing
You have to get away

You begin to fold
And refold
Creating layers of protection
Nothing but skin and innocence

The day comes
When you look at your parent
With the grave realization that
They are lost and
You do not have a net

You become more pragmatic
Than devout

Rubbing your own hope
Into your face
With the dry heels of your small hands
You explore
This new country
In which you now live

There is no vacation
From the irrational vigilance

That has no object
And grants no power

You trade away intimacy
For control

Finding warmth in the friction of relationships
Built past the childhood taken

You navigate
The jagged rocks

A world that would benefit
From hands that would do better to be idle

And it comes

A faint chant
Rising in volume
A sound devoid of pity

Finding residual illumination
From the refuse you are granted

Finding what no one wants
And creating a delicacy

Cardboard Sleds

I watch the children turn our summer hill into winter again.
They ride their cardboard boxes down our mound of sun-
    scorched grass.

I sit in my chair on the patio and swallow their joy.
The wonder in grass as snow and a sleigh ride
in shorts and a tee shirt.

The incongruity makes me smile
and elicits pealing giggles from these young souls.

Silly hill! Who knew that you could wear so many different
    coats?
Sliding through seasons and staying true to your childish
    purpose.
Slippery grass shining in the sun like the crystals of a frosty
    morning.

The children swerve down the elevation with abandon.
The climb back up is easier without the snow.

Legs languid in the heat.
Climbing the incline again and again.
Turning our slope into a sweaty mountain.

With each descending cascade the grass surrenders more dust.
As twilight approaches I finally call in the tumbling herd.

Not a Hero

My father was past 80 when he finally began to tell us
   about the war.
It was his first war, when he was only 20.
He served during three conflicts.
But it was that first war that marked him.

It started when we found the box of his medals and
we told him that he was a hero.
He became angry. He rejected the label with scorn.
He told us…

That he knew heroic men.
But that he was not one of them.
He said…

First you get scared and you stay scared.
You are frightened for so long and so relentlessly.

That you get angry and you stay angry.
You are angry for so long and so relentlessly.

That you get stupid.
You start to take risks.
You do crazy things that you would never have imagined.

And if those crazy things don't get you killed,
well then, they give you medals.

But it was all just because you were afraid.
And you didn't want to be there.
You could not believe that you WERE there.
How the hell did it happen?

You were pissed at yourself, and the enemy, and your
     mission,
and the cold, and the dirt and the bullets, and the
     goddam army!

He said the good war movies got a lot of it right.
At least the newer ones.
But he said they couldn't get at his deepest memory
     of it all.

The smell.

He told us of the smell of his own skin
and of the men around him in the foxholes.

Once they had a break.
The Major told them to put the torn and worn uniforms
     that they had been
wearing for months into a pile.
A gigantic pile of filthy fabric.
And they doused it with kerosene to burn the stench
     and the lice.
And they all got cold showers.
And fresh uniforms were on the way.

But the new uniforms never got there.

Each man had to pick through the pile of kerosene
    soaked garments.
Trying to find something close to the right size.
With correct rank and insignia.
He said he spent two more months in another man's
    clothes.
And that it took a week before the stink was his own
    again,
even through the stench of kerosene.
But they were grateful.
At least the fuel killed the lice.

He said the cold that winter was worse than the
    artillery.
The shells came in waves.
There were lulls and valleys in the action.
But the cold was constant.

He said you got worried if it stopped hurting.
That meant the cold was winning.
So you would shake and stomp to bring back the pain
that told you that you were still alive.

And then he showed us his three belly buttons from
    the bullet wounds.
But this time he wasn't being silly like every time before.
This time he was in earnest.
For the first time he was bearing witness.
It wasn't a punchline anymore.

He told us all of these things almost quietly.

Quickly, and with an embarrassment bordering on shame.
But also some stubborn pride.
He just wanted us to know.

That he was not a hero.
You see.

Into the Can (Haibun)

The small black kitten has been crushed, not yet quite dead. Her dark eyes are slits in her flattened face. Her white teeth are showing through her opened mouth, the tip of her pink tongue rests on the teeth, slightly protruding. She is trembling with small convulsions. I hold her in my 10 year old hands, ask my stepfather, almost pleading, if we can take her to the doctor. "No point", he says. "She's trash now, put her in the can outside." I walk up the steps from our basement apartment cradling the kitten in my upturned palms. I can still feel her trembling. I reach the heavy gray metal trash can. With the kitten in the crook of one arm, I pry off the frozen lid. I place the kitten onto the mound of cardboard and garbage in the can. It is twilight. Her black form lays on its side on the cardboard, like a charcoal cameo. I slowly replace the lid.

some need to grow thorns
to touch the pearl drop waters
part of me falls through

Crescent Moon Scars

I still see the vague echo of scars
on the inside of my forearm
where she gripped me
—her brightly colored nails
—biting into the flesh.

It is a form of love to want to control something
—no matter what the cost.

"Sit still and shut up!"

She needed me to do that
so her attention could focus
—on whatever man was the latest
—and ripe for the picking.

We were a team
—she would say
—harvesting the next meal ticket.

I hoped each man
and each scar
might earn me back
my bicycle.

Left in a storage bin
—near Bakersfield
—or maybe Riverside.

When we again sped the Mustang
—pell mell across the desert.
To a new place
where her face would also be new
and her stories would be believed.

Ladybug

"Ladybug, ladybug, fly away home.
Your house is on fire and your children will burn."
—English nursery rhyme

He didn't know what alcohol was,
except that it smelled sharp.

She mixed it with lemonade when she was alone,
on hot afternoons, with only him for company.

She called him her best buddy.
Hugged him close,
then pushed him away.

Blew cigarette smoke into his eyes
until they burned and he could not catch his breath.

When she wasn't sad or mad or drinking or crying,
they made jigsaw puzzles together.

She would remind him to find
all of the pieces with straight edges.

They would build the border,
fill it with all of the other pieces,
sorted by color and subject.

Part of a fence/
red like the bricks/
blue from the sky.

She was drinking this afternoon
and sent him outside with a grape popsicle.

She was tired of his questions.
Crying, because she had slapped him.

The sun was too warm on his face
as he sat in the dirt of the weed filled yard.

The popsicle was gone now.
He was getting thirsty.

A lady bug landed on the back
of his hand.

Sitting very still,
hoping she would not fly away,
he wanted to be her friend.

If he became very small or
she became very large,
they would fly away together.

They would make a new home for just the two of them.
It wasn't sad there.
It was quiet and calm.

They could go over the high fence,
Away from this dry choked place.
He would not be lonely.

But, now the ladybug seemed restless
and her wings fluttered.
He knew she was going to fly away.

He sat on the packed soil,
thirsty and afraid to go in.

His mother would yell.
Hold him down with her knees,
kneeling on his arms.

Tell him that it was all because of him.
That she too was lonely and trapped.

And, they were out of grape popsicles.

Kaddish (Ghazal)

The ten old men sit side-by-side comparing death.
Say, we grow warm—the planet now is sharing death.

Say, with each new storm and flood the wounds grow deeper.
While neighbors turn their heads away—just daring death.

No masks—no shots—the death toll just keeps rising, so
these men know, there's no point to try despairing death.

They make their peace in any soil that they find.
And know there is no stake in us foreswearing death.

The ten old men (begin to chant) their Kaddish now.
Lament to face a stern and quite uncaring death.

They sing to all the things that we are losing now.
A song of faith that brings us to unerring death.

The old men call to bees— and to the buffalo.
They chant (for all the things) that will be wearing death.

The content of old men's hearts—inform their prayers.
They try to guard themselves from known impending death.

They wish for all, and pray for each, escape from death.
Pray—(add my name) to chanting for lamenting death.

We Both Like Oranges.

It was not crowded in the Primate House
at the National Zoo that day.
She caught my eye through the low window
from several feet away.

Her large brown eyes held a calmness and, sturdiness.
This female orangutan was looking in at all of us.
Today she was people-watching.
She beckoned me over to where she was sitting.

Her hands moved with purpose as I approached.
I had learned some limited sign language
working with kids at the rehab center.
I walked up to the glass and crouched to face her.

"What is your name?" she signed.
I finger spelled my name. Four letters.
She watched my hand intently
and indicated that she wanted me to repeat the gestures.

After four or five times she spelled my name back to me
and pointed to me pleased that I had now been labeled
and identified. She looked at me with expectation.
I realized that it was my turn.

"What is your name?" I signed.

She made the sign for flower or blossom.
I dubbed her Rosy on the spot.

She pointed toward my two toddlers who were
wandering behind me.

She asked if they were mine. I indicated yes
and she pointed toward each,
making the signs, boy?...girl? I nodded.
She seemed satisfied and pointed behind herself.

She indicated that she had a daughter who was napping.
Hidden from view in the habitat and not available for
    introduction.
It was as if we were neighbors becoming acquainted
across the fence that separated our yards.

Her huge eyes were almost golden—and patient,
as she signed, "What do you like to eat?"
I knew she was a vegetarian.
I made the sign for fruit.

That seemed right.
She sat and thought for a moment
and then told me with her hands
that she was partial to oranges.

I said, "me too!" We looked into each other's eyes
astounded by the connection. In wonder of our
    sameness
through the thickened glass
and past a sea of difference.

She appeared to hear something behind her in the habitat.
She rose while maintaining eye contact.

Then she held up her hand in farewell
while still gazing into my eyes.

We shared the planet together for three breaths.
She ambled away back into her habitat.
I watched her wide back recede into the tree-filled tableau
across so much disparity of experience.

The Universe Is Porous And Osmosis Creates A Bleeding

You locked us in our attic bedroom
on nights when you wanted to have sex.

We had to pee in the toy box.
I blamed it on the cat.

We all leak slightly. We all
resist looking at the stain.

At fourteen, I stopped your swinging
stinging slap.

As I caught your wrist in my palm
mid-swing, I saw in your eyes

what you thought you had made.
The punished child becomes

every man who has ever struck you.
Your blows had won, you thought.

I dropped your hand.
I was not your sin eater.

I would not be your sin.

James D'Agostino

James D'Agostino is the author of *Nude With Anything* (New Issues Press), *The Goldfinch Caution Tapes*, winner of the 2022 Anthony Hecht Prize (Waywiser Press), and three chapbooks which won prizes from Diagram/New Michigan, CutBank Books, and Wells College Press. His chapbook, *Gorilla by Jellyfish Light*, is forthcoming from Seven Kitchens Press. His poems have appeared in *Ninth Letter, Forklift Ohio, Conduit, Mississippi Review, Bear Review, TriQuarterly, Laurel Review*, and elsewhere. He teaches at Truman State University, lives in Missouri and Iowa City, IA, with his partner, the poet and book artist Karen Carcia.

The Ear Speaks

In this 20 degree last week of February
lake ice gets elastic as it suns and heats.

It's one big sheet of tin, warbling storm
sound effects for an old radio drama.

19 Nocturne Boulevard. 33 Half Moon St.
It's kinda creature feature, this theremin

I'm in again in the rhythm of my dead
dog's bad dreams, that whimper bubbled

up from some sleep's deep. The Cinnimon
Bear. The American Forum of the Air.

Bi-plane buzz past. Stock car wave crash.
It's also slowly bovine. It's the ghost

lowing of every $1 Double we passed
in the pasture. Lagoon is what it says

or wants to. Point is it's the only thing
I've heard in a while made any sense

and it's not going to last. Accordiana.
Blue Beetle. Blue streak of talked-up sky

above this warming study in sound
dispersion: how frequencies fray,

sequence, fire a little laser pistol, a little
bit of whistle that the higher hertz

arrive with. The lower get here later,
glissando down through sad glass and,

as all old songs gloss loss, you're glad
you're here to hear it.

Quantum Tantrum

At one point in development
Pac-Man was Chompsky.
The week I was born
the number one song

was Send in the Clowns.
End of Feb the first half
inch of daffodils don't defile
a thing. They say we are

twenty days ahead toward
Spring which almost gets us
whole. We're three weeks
late with everything, but

whatever little purple vents
the violets opened in the earth
must've done their work
b/c one dove on the phone

line blows its pop bottle
vowel and just like that
we're all still here. A mile-off
vulture slow scoots its cone

of carrion scan and I could
care less more often which
is just boredom and a big
problem. Bigger still there

might not be a single poem
in it, but the job's work
the spine of the notebook,
strengthen your core. Pry,

encrypted ear, a prayer.
Day goon, yon god dog,
do agony. Nod and go
your life is any good yo.

How Not to Float Off Into Space

If you're not down here
tangled in the names of things
sit very still. Only look at
what makes you notice. Once
it's low enough to ripple over
pebbles, the creek face gets
a rib cage, and even a cursory
review of extant lit swears
a heart's not far behind.
What a find, might not match
JR's arrowheads and blow dart
bone, but still I'm silt-soaked,
still got all bit up, climbed
back out with this orange
jewel weed. Good days
you go for your phone and
it's not there so you pat
your pocket, now your body's
got to be the camera, and that
blink right there's your shutter
speed, and there—what a body
of work!—luckily a film of silver
lines the inside of your skull
so the pluses blooming further
into asterisks on the vine stay
little Phillips heads that leave
a lot of nicks in the photo plate

named sweet autumn clematis,
the one we're all trapped in
again, trying to make room,
ballooning over tombs.

Last Sunday of Summer

We're a part of this harvest
moon never mind the cloud
cover. That cardinal clinking
coins. I'm always three pages
away, troubled, but with
measurables. Walnut thumps
come between smaller
and smaller slices of silence.
Lately it's not light and dark,
it's light and lit, whole shadows
of it, even though today
the drear reared word-ward,
drew weird birds. That's no way
to write's the way to, too.
I mean you buy it, you break it.
Had a kid in my office tell me
he's been told he's romantic
lead or shark of a lawyer,
so I gave him Anne Carson
only until Thursday. Another
one told me he couldn't take
anything out of his poem
because he's already lost so
much, so I told him come back
later for Anne Carson. Who'd
say to a sunrise I know skies
who do what you do only way

way better? Pierce the crepe
of experience and out gurgles
nice ripe nectarine light,
well, it might. Poet, go on
the g, not on the o.

—for Dean Young
1955-2022

Peace Troika for Ukraine

Poem for Volodymyr Zelensky (Beginning and Ending with Endings by John Murillo)

"If the traitor, language, is not to be exiled, one may disarm him and make him a prisoner of war."
> —Barbara Hernstein Smith, Poetic Closure

You dream of stockpiles—
bottles filled with gas,

the mid-writhe rebar rubble
of an unreadable alphabet

in unseeable cities. All
too. Look

for yourself. Seen
from space the line

of tanks' slowly-threaded dread
treads toward the capital.

There are nearly 45 miles
of nerves running through

the body. Please.
Come closer.

Take this from my hand.

Nativity as Pietà

"That's how Fakenews is born."
—Dmitry Polyansky, First Deputy Permanent Representative
of Russia to the UN

no windows so the snow is
glass before it lands

steam from the sloughed-off
face of the hospital bombed

the pregnant mother stretchered
out atop a strawberry blanket

hauled from inside in between
the ash heaps in between her

breathing who says to the medics
when she learned her baby

wouldn't live kill me now has
died and in between breaths

the UN rep from Russia says
this hospital has been turned

into a military object bombed
in between his cease and fire in

between an acre of land 50,000
pounds of strawberries can grow

which aren't they called by how
carefully they're held above

the dirt by straw by hand

The Bombing of Art School No. 12

—Georgy Senchenko

If you could say it in the words I saw
the angel in the marble and carved until

I set him free, there'd be no reason to
make your shadow darker closer toward its

origin, and at its end transformed to
light. Things disappear. If you want to see

anything, you are going to have to
hurry. You must close your eyes, sing things

we have no words for—picture, history,
and other people—the artist is like

an abuser of everything, which makes
art inevitable. A ribbon around

a bomb. It's what you get away. Only it
can do it. Every shelter's makeshift.

Reading Spoon River Anthology
in a Small-Town Cemetery

1.

Teeth

Ovate to heart-shaped
like the leaves of linden,
best in late May, but

who isn't? The dove /
laundry / handkerchief /
ghost tree slowly teethes

the headstone of Ralph P.
I don't know what to do
about knowing that.

2.

Lucy Joe and Lark

Katydids and crickets socket different
wrenches in two different directions

and call it summer song, call it see
if that'll hold, call it back to school

anthem for Lucy Joe and Lark, called
back 1942 and '48, and let the breeze

plink up in the leaves behind. Died
poorer, died sooner. The smaller

the headstone the lower the toppling odds
and, toppled gods, the Watsons

got that strawberry graphite marble
marker, how it looks in just a little

snow, furred meat in a free fall, oak so
thick and tall even leafless there's

enough trunk limb branch and twig
to keep your light at most diffused,

which like our railroad, long-removed,
lives on—not a phantom limb, a photon,

but a line you find, a hallway halfway
bindweed, halfway sky in which

a read-by-me moon rises, coming
freight, a paper lantern poised

in plowed-through tree boughs,
ghost horn calling all night long.

3.

Negative Ease

These three degrees
below mornings'

light through the oaks
throw shadows

down the steep slope
of our cemetery hill, whole

trees laid bare
like an X-ray

of the non-compete
clause in the long

-standing agreement
between roots

and graves, leaves
and left.

Vulture Moon

I dreamed a bear and a couple cubs up
the street but woke to buzzards. The best part

of six buzzards at the dregs edge of this
little drained pond's the three still in the sky.

Cadaverous kites catch this June morning
wind and I'll never get their shadows right.

A vulture moon dissolves into the blue.
The blotlight sweeps through the trees. No. Night runs

its fingers through the leaves. No. A slow-beam
darker flicker I still don't have. Not yet.

Bear-colored, flesh-red face, denuded bone
a rotted cone of moonlight chewed, this

slivered-almond beak that eats and eats
the only road home again clean.

Reading Ada Limón While Down the Hall, Out the Window, One Story Down

Two dead birds, maybe
window-bonked, maybe

hawk-toppled nest
or flying lesson

snuffed all at once
for the fully-fledged

and fledgling, both,
a cardinal and a could

have been, an Audubon
abandoned flat on the tar

paper of the University
President's entrance overhang.

All flight is controlled
falling, windspeed

and snappable bone, so
hollow you could breathe

through, play its minute
flute to this dance

macabre, to sing clear
through to the other side.

Patricia Cleary Miller

Patricia Cleary Miller is amused and amazed by the strange people she sees in her placid town, but she dares not write about them--you might recognize them. Patricia taught literature and writing at Rockhurst University, and now she is helping to raise money for students majoring in the Humanities. Her poems and biographical musings have appeared in many journals, including *New Letters, The Same, I-70 Review, Helicon Nine,* and *Connecticut Review.* Her poetry collection, *Starting a Swan Dive*, published by BKMK Press, won the Daniel S. Brenner Award for Scholarly Achievement. Her book *Crimson Lights* collected the poems she wrote as poet laureate of the Harvard Alumni Association 2004-2012. Her latest collection, *Can You Smell the Rain?* is available from BkMk Press

Rice

(for Judith Thompson and Arn Chorn)

I bend over, pick the rice, rice is good,
I eat rice, bend over, pick the rice pick plop
rice sticks in water in light my face in water
rice is good, rice sticks, rice sticky,
Mother Father I pick, steam, eat rice.
Buddha's soft face, my face in the water.
Mother Father Buddha eat rice.

I give Him my bowl, my pomegranate,
the jewels of the Lord God Buddha dance on the water.
I am a drop of water in the sea in Buddha I am water,
I dip my hand in and out of water, hold the sunlight
hold the jewels of rice and water and light,
the heart of light, palm fronds, coconut, date,
waxy leaves, sparkling lizards, rice.

Mekong, Yangtze, Ganges, Tigris, Euphrates, Mississippi
rice, corn, beans, peanuts, tobacco, sugar palm, salt.
Sandstone Buddhas. My fields are prey to Siam. Annam.
France. Japan. Viet Nam. Pol Pot.
A club misses my head, Mother slips in water
blood in water, water bugs in light

Father shot in green leaves, uncles brothers
dragged from hut, sisters aunts starve slowly
in the sunlight, bullets skim my chest.
Bayonets rip my body, soldiers eat my kidneys
one after the other while I still live.

Sandstone columns lurch, Buddha topples.
The Lord God splinters, shatters on red tiles,
children's wails claw my temple walls.
Stars rise like jewels.

Budapest Street Scene

Two sisters in father's new car

Those girls were alive.
> *Yes, we'll get your Porsche home by midnight.*
> *We're going to the Portside Bar. All our friends go there.*
> *We love the Cuban music.*

They met university students from Munich.
They drank Golden Pheasant Slovak beer.
They sang, they danced, they planned a picnic at the zoo
    tomorrow.
All those cute boys, the summer breeze,
The girls' darling little skirts and spike-heeled sandals.
Those girls were alive.

One boy said,
> *Last spring a girl disappeared from the Portside Bar.*
> *After a while, the police stopped looking.*
> *The parents came in from Rumania.*
> *Heavy equipment dredges the Danube.*
> *They found her two kilometers downriver from the Chain Bridge.*

It was late, but not that late.
But they hurried home along Vaci Street,
heading for the Elizabeth Bridge, to Kossuth Lajos Street.
It was late but not too late.

The utility pole came out of nowhere.
The flames came out of nowhere.
The paramedics tried to open the doors.
The flames came out of nowhere.
The paramedics tried.
It was late but not that late.
Those girls were alive.

Chris Norman, Small Bagpipes

Chris Norman, small bagpipes green velvet,
drone, low drone, whine, start melody,
stomp heel, stomp terrazzo floor --

Cynthia taps her fingers, claps her hands,
drums her palm on red silk skirt, pianos her fingers,
drums faster taps faster, everyone vibrating stomping,
Ellen's face is aglow and Rick is bobbing his head up
and down and electric currents pulse out the top of my head.

    These Celts, my ancestors, danced on the highlands.
    Mother's hair was red and she danced on the hills.
    electricity sparks out the top of my head, tapping
    tapping, my auburn-haired mother dances dances.

    Not Cromwell, but Bonnie Prince Charlie --
    Thomas Kelton: down up the hill, feint.
    Mayhem. Surrounded. Captured.
    Deported. Many died on the ship
    to Lynn, Massachusetts iron works.
    Oh please, my Celtic ancestor, live
    long enough to reproduce.

Cynthia keeps clapping and Ellen's face is aglow,
and Rick is bobbing his head up and down,
and we are all tapping and tapping and stomping
and drinking single malt with nary a splash of water,
and we are all stomping and tapping and Chris looks
mesmerized and everyone has gone into a reverie.

Oh Mother with red hair,
where are you now?
Please oh please be dancing on the hills.
Mother why did you cut your hair,
dye it black? Why did you die?

Lilies

Easter lilies, rubrum lilies, trumpet her perfection,
thornless roses drape her body, protecting my Madonna.
Rose satin hides the wooden bier, doves coo in silver cages;
she watches bluebirds soaring free across the painted ceiling.

We've brushed the green silk draperies, polished the walnut
    paneling with beeswax.
In the parlour where I keep vigil night after night, I will her
    flowers
To stay fresh forever, I will her to live. She will stay here with
    me, and each day
I will add more lilies and roses. While they perfume the air,
    she abides with me.

But the flowers flow backward to their source, they sphacelate.
Before they liquefy, I will dip each one in white wax,
Layer after layer, fresh forever; still perfumed, she lives.

Lovely and lively, all covered with lilies,
I keep my Madonna, she flies from her cage –
We soar to the heavens with bluebirds and doves.

Nonce sonnet written in Response to Above and Beneath the
Skin, A Retrospective Exhibition of the Works of Petah Coyne,
Organized by the Albright-Knox Art Gallery in Buffalo, New
York; At the Kemper Museum of Contemporary Art, Kansas
City, Missouri, 16 September through 27 November 2005.

Petah Coyne tells of an old Irish funeral custom of laying out the beloved in the parlor and covering the body with a blanket of flowers; as the flowers decayed, the family would add more and more flowers; eventually there would be a putrid mess. To memorialize and transform this custom, Coyne constructs sculptures from masses of stuffed birds and silk flowers that she covers with some two dozen layers of black or white wax. In some of her sculptures she hides the face and praying hands of a plastic Madonna.

Ship Burial

(after Amaryllis, 1980, by Frances Cohen Gillespie)

If my amaryllis blooms, my crystal cross
and perfume bottles will glow red,
will dance in the sunlight.
Sparkles will fill my millefiori room

But the painted amaryllis lean out at me,
they loom over the fallen flower in the dragon vase;
the blue dragon vase with barking mouth,
Scyld Sheafson's burial ship.

That Good King sails over thick brocade waves,
the black silk sea obstructed by golden flowers,
golden iceberg calves; the Dragon Ship barks.
Mired in the clotting golden flowers,
the dragon ship cannot reach the looming potted plant.

Today and forever the flowers suck up all the air;
the flowers will never wither,
the dragon ship will never be alone
and safe upon the brocade sea.

Mother Won't Buy Polypropylene

Mother was invited skiing.
I tell her about polypropylene.
She calls it polygamy-ethylene-acetylene.
I give her a fuzzy blue ear band,
loan her my black hood.
She says, "I'll look like a terrorist."
I send her out for a parka.
"You can't ski in mink," I say.
"What would Catherine Deneuve wear?" she asks.
She insists the geese in my down coat are dead.
She comes back with a yellow cashmere sweater.
"On sale it cost about the same as polyethylene," she says.
"Those Tibetan goats are still alive," she says."
I send her out for jerseys and long johns.
She comes back with a gold jacket.
"I'm old enough for gold lame."
I ask, "Where will you wear it?"
She says, "It brightens up my apartment.
I might ask some people over.
I can wear it to the movies."

Mother Won't Wear Walking Shoes

"He had patterns that had been cut through
like the windows of Saint Paul's in either shoe."

--Chaucer, "The Miller's Tale"

Mother won't wear walking shoes.
Her topaz and ruby heels spike
in gratings, shred on brick sidewalks.
I show her Bally flats, Adidas;
she says, "Henry won't love me
shod like that."
Her calves are matchsticks.
I point to wheelchairs.
She says, "I tuck under,
my legs are steel."
She silicones amethyst suede platforms,
disdains my LL Bean boat shoes.
Her boots, laced high,
have patterns cut through like cathedral windows.
She says, "Henry told me,
'Don't buy shoes without me.'"
I say, "He's in London."
She says, "He'll know.
He's buying me slippers
to sip champagne from."

As the Firefly Passes through Flame

after Saint Francis de Sales, Introduction to the Devout Life, 1609
sonnet for the inauguration of a university president
To study is a good way to learn; to hear is a still better way;
but to teach is the best of all. --Erasmus
The office of teaching serves as a foundation for learning. --St. Augustine

As the firefly passes through the flames and does
not singe its wings; as the pearl oyster flourishes
in the fresh spring in the midst of the salt sea,
so you, oh Philothea, my child in love with God,
may live Devoutly in towns, in families, at court,
in the mechanic's shop, and on the battlefield.

The florist arranges bouquets in vast variety;
with His many voices, the Spirit inspires His children,
loves His wild array of blooms – His mechanics
and teachers and soldiers.

    Every colored jewel
shines brighter when coated in honey, as your life,
    Philothea,
gains luster through Devotion.

    In study, hearing,
teaching, you may shine through honey, fly
through flames, find fresh water in the sea.

At That Moment

At that very moment, my fingers were claws of light,
Lasers, long, cutting the air, floating
on the ends of my hands, white light, yellow
blue white. Pointing, they lit, not scraped,
not cut, *illuminated* your face, slid over,
smoothed your face, fluffed and curled your hair.
White light up to stars, the stars shooting
whirling, spinning, sifting floating down.

And in the crook of your neck, the hollow of your shoulder,
where my face rests, where I kiss your hard strong flesh,
inhale your scent, I pull back my face, jerk up
my neck; and in the hollow dark, light streaking
its shadows, a small friendly bat face, like a plush
rabbit's; like my bat ring: the Chinese man said,
"That bat is blind." This bat is soft and kindly,
dark in the hollow of your neck, and I pull my face
back out of the hollow, and the bat face is light all white
and golden. And I scream and you hold me, clutch me hard.
Yes. Oh, Baby, and Yes, we laugh, yes YES.

I Ask the Little Prince about Yellow Roses

*If you love a flower that lives on a star, it is sweet to look at the sky at night.
All the stars are   abloom with flowers.*

--Antoine de Saint Exupéry, The Little Prince

Can the flower bloom in the desert?
How does it?
With her four thorns, can she defend herself
against the blazing sun?
Too much
not enough
rain.

Must there be color?
Can black and white film show a flower
if the flower is white?

If you snarl at a flower
will it wither and crumble?

Only one bouquet per room now.
Long-stemmed yellow roses at dinner.

Why breed roses for color alone?
We must have perfume
in every room
and in the garden
and in the woods
and in the stars.

Jose Faus

José Faus is writer, performer and visual artist. He is a founder of the Latino Writers Collective and sits on the boards of The Latino Writers Collective and Charlotte Street Foundation. His writing appears in numerous anthologies. His chapbook *This Town Like That* was released by Spartan Press. His second book of poetry *The Life and Times of Jose Calderon* was published by West 39 Press.

Invasion

The pigeons bring tidings of another war
Refugee messages circle the blank-eyed cities
They would have been here sooner
but the cannonade buckled latitude
and longitude to arbitrary nodes

Unwrap the gauze lightly from the pigeon's legs
lay it flat on the table study the contours
dark edges lines the sacred text of plans
the weight of metal tracks
the metronome for melodies
of bleating trumpets

Converging planes and lines defile snow-draped fields
There is nothing new to see here or there
nothing memorializes what is readily forgotten
no monuments consecrate what was never sacred

There is no fog but a shimmering night
glimpses defining the topography of death
edicts now gray slabs and coils of iron bar
crystalized concrete in the glean of a cold moon
erased bodies fertilize the hollow ground
as a flag whips high above collapsed halls

Flags embossed on caissons pulled by mules
arrive from the cardinal directions
The sun sets again on this whirligig
You have seen them all your life
prepare your children to see them
transparent as branches in
March April and May

What is new now that yesterday wasn't full of
What will be tomorrow that was not enough today

Quarantine dirge

A Bell rings over grey streets half empty neighborhoods
Desolate doors fall nudged by the slighted breeze
The sidewalks break slabs torn asunder push skyward
forced by exhaling inhaling roots of ash and sycamores
shriveled leaves twirl about rusting iron fences
the spirits of the composed roam unimpeded
dance macabre jigs of grace and death
above weed filled graves and souring odes

while the gates clang against broken hasps
sermons fill the sky like sparrows in a death spiral
hurtling earthward homilies and hosannas
epitaphs and skeins of wine and penitence
not enough to quell the groans of hospital wards
trailer park morgues and the loud chants of no
bouncing off dusty books and nursery rhymes

Details of the crime are in the margins
Cliff notes to an apocalypse broadcast
like moldy fishing nets cast certain
of one last catch before unraveling
The din of impenitent voices
clamor above babbling rebukes
As rains pound the band plays
a host of nocturnes and lullabies

The spaniel chases its tail the length of the sidewalk
The cat licks the same paw as the post man
repeats his route again and again
to the clang of a salvation army bell

Moorish moon

Hooves pound the ground
convulse vibrate
spirited quavers
restless in a diminishing
prismatic light

Primal snorts
ruffle the calm
the blue city
light and mountains

In the creeping dimness
the purple outlines of
banded horsemen
cross legged on carpets
sheathed knifes on laps
suffer quietly
sip their tea
beneath the indigo dusk
the sullen moon

They shelter
among the dunes
as a cool breeze dithers
across a blue black pond
while the buffet of hooves
stirs an evolving
achromatic night

Build

Night's violet edge
dissolves corners
beams windows
stairs and dormers

Joists collapse
sill plates shatter
purple overcomes
a house in the dunes

Flicks of light
align with stars
dissipate as desert
mimics crimson blue

Memories release ballast
float up down
travel sideways
a frail permanence migrates
along raked floors
and shifting walls

Night is an incessant beat
a flat staff sheltering
the melody of a collapsing house

While a minor chord
holds day's last breath
a sigh cries indigo

Para morir hay que vivir

(On seeing Jean Basquiat's Bird on Money)

Mad dash be-bopping
Yardbird in flight
salt peanuts salt peanuts
the first breath first mark
first step first flap first sigh

Bird on money tada
Fingers caress
a one note sustain
Dervish fingers pray
we'll see the domes of
Tunisia before light

Arrows fletched chicken scratch
teal that thing you do before blue
and black turn purple and orange
Tossed swinging ecstatic
comet burning high stepping

Para morir hay que sufrir
A green wood haze
On the way to the grave
stop create

The Widow Cardona

It was in the first embrace
the warm night's bare chest
muscles beneath Orion's belt
a spark taut and so perfect
she traced filigrees and curly cues
with her tongue along his breast
then sewed them on her scarf

The gallop ended at the fence post
a barb in hand the trot home
the bundled sweat-filled day
the firm snap of the strap
across the barely opened bag
the hand on the shoulder
the wordless goodbye

The corners are tucked
neat on his side of the bed
The riding crop wrapped about
the ear of the stile marries
the clean spindles of his chair

She holds the scarf
tight about her neck
stiff like the folds of her coat

In reflection she sees shadows
from crystal candle stems
She holds the switch
but dares not
turn on the light

Riotous

Don't let me walk
or tread lightly
on anything
not when the wind gusts
and calls my name
I want the letters
bouncing off the walls
and many doors
I have walked past
I want to run barefoot
through shards
fly blind like birds
skimming moonless waters
I want to stir the flatness
and ripple waves
I want to tilt a boat
swamp a skirt
love under a burning moon
howl wolf at everything
and nothing the way
waves pound on rocks
my song an insatiable cicada
I want the briny sugar of love
on my tongue and lips
the rim of the cup I drink
and the rough winds on my skin

No mast when the sirens sing
I want to drown in their arms
and sing lullabies in a deep bass
that shakes up tsunamis
pendulums infinitely swinging
leaving meridians a shambles
no transgressions regressions
conceits apologies or tears
just the cacophony of yes

Mood Gemini

For Elijah McClain

Breathing is the easiest thing I do
Thousands of times a day
I take my allotted breaths
Is there a proper way to do it
I am not familiar with
Because I would do it if
it made the world a better place
I take deep breaths
when my music plays
measure steps like beats
walk a straight path
at times meander
smell a flower shake my limbs
step aside and let flies be
twirl and shake to the songs I see

No offense but
I think I breathe the way
I am meant to sing

I walk alone but I'm never lonely
We all walk alone don't we?
But my walk is not a sad song
I always know where I mean to go
Tonight I am walking home
Isn't that all we mean to do
make it back one more time
before the moon declines

I have a card identifies me
Say my name please just once
That is me let me introduce myself
"My name is Elijah McClain.
I'm an introvert. I'm just different. That's all.
I'm so sorry. I have no gun. I don't do that stuff.
 I don't do any fighting. Why are you attacking me?
I don't even kill flies! I don't eat meat!
But I don't judge people,
I don't judge people who do eat meat.
Forgive me. All I was trying to do was become better.
I will do it. I will do anything. Sacrifice my identity, I'll do it.

But it is getting harder to breathe
Is there a better way
Cause I will do it if it will
make the world a safer space
Tonight seems the wrong time to ask
I was almost home
Listen
Listen to the song I was singing
Listen please listen
I can't breathe
and it is the easiest thing I do
the easiest thing I do
I hear you breathing
I just can't breathe correctly
like you
so easily
do

A poet died tonight

A poet died tonight
No one cried
just yawns from passersby
and a whistle like the squeal
of a toy truck backing up

No premonitions or mysteries
learned astronomers to sing
constellations to sail by
just the sun going down
and the moon lining up
while stars flicker in the sky

Cats beneath halogen lamps
lick their paws
haunches on garbage cans
Dogs howl at empty chicken coops
sleep in padlocked yards

A woman pulls a curtain open
on a corner flat above a diner
looks down the street
whispers a prayer to the dark
seals the window tight
No finger clutching diamonds
No expectations no regrets
only the rustle of the curtain
scraping the weathered jamb

Death is death and life is death
No one cares enough to ask
No news in letters to decipher
Armies line up and shoot
Soldiers take breaths and die
No hearse or attendants on call
just the usual profligates to reward
No way to tell a red wheelbarrow
from a crushed yellow cadillac
No month crueler than any other
A fork in the road is two roads
no consequence in retelling
A clock ticks an ordained time
Wheels turn from the effort of a crank
Fortunata's wheel breaks
and we wander blind

Nothing happens anymore
A poet died tonight
and the barred owl
circled the collapsing barn
clutched the peak above the gate
and fell asleep

For Francisco Alarcon

On this cold December night
the words drop on the paper
easy as the light
from the sliver of moon
hovering over these lands
where Hopi Navajo Anasazi
dwell off the side of cliffs
drawing the breath
in fits and gasps
like the first laugh of a child
where coyote crosses roads
near first second and third mesas
and the old villages mirroring
the belt and heft of Orion
I see you shaman
with the spark of your eye
drawing us closer
to the gathering places
the waves of your hair
strands ladders to the old tales
and sacred halls of Cibola
Aztlan Quivira and Eldorado
Set the dinner before us
there are many to feed
as your children come
for the final blessing
once more before
turtle glides to the bottom
Previously published on Poetry Bay

Tina Hacker

Tina Hacker's newest poetry collection is *GOLEMS*, published by Kelsay Books. The poems are based on the magical mud and clay creature from Jewish folklore who is conjured from the earth to accomplish a task. After fulfilling it and often having a good time, the golem returns to the earth. Tina has authored two previous collections of poetry: *Listening to Night Whistles* published by Aldrich Press and *Cutting It*, by The Lives You Touch Publications. In 2016 Tina was named a Muse of The Writers Place in Kansas City, MO, and serves as the poetry editor for *Veterans' Voices*, a national magazine of writing by military veterans. She has been nominated for a Pushcart Prize four times.

Looking for Helen

"The worst part was the hunger."
My cousin Helen says this
about her time at Auschwitz.
It's all she'll say. She pretends not to hear
my pleas for more information,
lapses into Hungarian, fleeing to the words
of her youth and remaining there
until the all clear is sounded
by talk of other matters, other times.

I hear rabbis repeat reasons why Helen
should, must, ought to say more.
"For future generations, for past generations,
for all generations."
They smile at her, confident in their skills
at persuasion until they feel
gusts of her silence, hear the trumpet call
of her unspoken words sound retreat.

I can now meet with Helen
without asking about the camp.
I ignore the restless questions,
tossing and turning in my mind,
catch them before they lunge at her
with impatient demands. Each year,
the unease becomes easier to bear.

But last month, when I called Helen's office,
a voice hollow with indifference said,
"No one by that name works here.
Maybe Julie can help you?"
My cousin came on the line.
She told me her real name was Julie,
and didn't know why the family always
called her Helen. That's all she'd say.

I can now call her Julie without translating
her new name into the original.
I wonder if she will change her name again.
Where has she put Helen?
Is she in hiding so when the Nazis
come, her neighbors will say,
"No one by that name lives here."

Sheba

In one of the last days of summer,
in a last hour of the day,
when minutes begin to liquefy
and flow to the earth
like thick syrup,
she stood in the doorway
and inhaled
the scent of leaves and grass
drifting through the air,
a tang of death blurring the edges
of the aroma,
fogging the last bits of spice
released by the summer sun.
She lingered in front of the
screened door
listening to cicadas
struggle against their dying,
protesting oblivion.
A turban covered
some sparse strands of her hair,
left after the second round of chemo,
a few curling strands stubbornly clinging
to her scalp like cut roses
cleaving to color and fragrance.
Like Sheba, she looked regal
in her headdress and robe,
straight and strong

to the passerby,

her mind not ready to answer

the question facing

the moth circling the light above her head.

Counting Peas

Lydia's mother counted the peas
she put on every plate. Twenty.
No seconds allowed.
More than she found on her plate
during the Great Depression.
Her girlhood pinched her face,
left her eyes in a squint.
She worried that Lydia would
forget her stories
about one meal a day,
shoes with paper linings.

The stories Lydia heard
were like a sweater
she couldn't wait to take off.
She gave her children
all the food they wanted,
enjoyed tossing leftovers
down the disposal.

In today's Maybe Recession,
Maybe Depression,
Lydia pushes her fears back
like Sisyphus as she watches
her 401K disappear into the ether.
She hears her son tell her grandson
that last year's sneakers can't possibly pinch,
that the hot dogs taste as good
as the ones his wife used to buy.

Listening to Southern Women

My friends' words amble toward me in sentences
brimming with leisure and graceful as a gauzy summer
  dress.
We are four women having coffee on a warm Alabama
  morning,
and I am a guest from Chicago sharing the comfort of
  caffeine.

My conversation is like a strand of glass beads,
each word tightly tied to the other, a string of plosive
  sounds.
I pause to breathe, every thought in place, and wait for
  a reply.

Their words undulate close to me, browsing the beads.
They hold up one and then another.
The women's thoughts glide over mine with unhurried
  ease
as they consider and savor my meaning,
taking time to sip some coffee,
to admire the garden, to pause before moving on.

My mouth opens and words rush out
to fill each second of their silence.
I complete their sentences, guess conclusions.
My sentences push and pull.
Theirs wait with polite patience.

While I struggle into stillness, a cat stretches at my feet.
And once more, the humid air around me
fills with the strolling interplay
of words and ideas that find time sweet.

Hiding Places

Some survived because they hid
behind false walls, in secret attics,
under floors in pits the Nazis missed.

When I was a child, I hid inside a shadow
when obliging drapes held sunlight
at bay. I felt invisible except Mother

always found me. Sometimes angry,
she'd ask, "Why didn't you come
when I called?" I wouldn't answer.

I hoped my stillness would shimmer
like a mirage, blurring me until
I was sure I was safe. I never knew

when I was safe. In my first apartment
I looked for a place. Bent down to peer
under our bed. Too childish, too obvious.

I pushed our large recliner into a corner
and crouched behind. A tweed grizzly
guarding my cave, but its hulking body

left revealing gaps. Maybe bury myself
beneath piles of pillows, become invisible
under shams, throws, bolsters on our bed.

My husband said I was silly. This is America.
Can't happen here. But I never knew
when I was safe, could never feel safe enough.

Halloween is three weeks away. Bottles
of false blood, elastic gore, plastic wounds
from vampires, zombies, maybe Nazis

line shelves. Make-believe fatal wounds.
Look bloody, look repulsive, look dead, I thought.
Lie very still, hide in plain sight.

The Ninotchka Syndrome

We always knew Ninotchka
would come over to our side.
Garbo, with a Russian accent
thick as her eyebrows were thin,
struck languid poses that belied
her stiff soldier's uniform.
Though all those brass buttons
were chic in '39,
we knew the moment
she slipped silk over her shoulders
and sipped champagne at the Ritz,
her resolve would break quicker than
a stiletto caught in a grate
on the Champs-Élysées.
And we can't forget Mel Douglas,
oozing enough charm to butter rye
for all the peasants in Moscow.
We always knew Ninotchka
was no fluke. After all,
she lived happily ever after,
like the generations of immigrants
France greeted, England greeted,
Liberty greeted. We always knew
the charms of Western culture
could disarm anyone until nineteen men
savored their last lap dance,
took a final stroll through Walmart,
watched one more movie on cable,
and found two towers easy prey.

Death of a Gucci Handbag

Within a week.
Dropped inside the bag during a showing
of *Out of Africa,* buttery popcorn
liquefies words scribbled
on scraps of paper scattered on the bottom.
Gumbo of oil and ink
permanently tattoo the cotton jacquard lining.

Within two weeks.
Stuffed with books
and rubber-banded slabs of coupons
on the edge of expiration,
the bag bulges and swells
like a can of rotting tomatoes.
Tissue nests choke zippers,
leaving toothy yawns.

Within three weeks.
Swung at a spider crawling up
the wall, the strap fractures.
Safety pins come to the rescue,
pierce, connect, but hold steadfast
until the holes expand,
explode into crevices
that split the strap end to end.

The death.

Money-back-guaranteed
leather cleaners ignore scrapes
as they slide over them.
Gucci pattern mimics peeling sunburn
under the onslaught of cleanser
and before a tribunal in the garbage can
testifies to the bag's demise.

Where Are You, Merle Oberon?

Your name eluded me
just as you eluded poor Olivier,
made him chase your skirts across the moors.
I ran after, wresting images from *Wuthering Heights*
of heather and smoky hearths,
but not your name. I saw you so clearly,
your impossibly smooth skin,
your oh-so-genteel accent,
your brown eyes tilted slightly at the edges.
But your name evaded me, a vexing specter
treading shallows, diving then surfacing,
showing a tempting syllable of arm, a suffix of shoulder.
Did Heathcliff, standing at the edge
of a fog-cloaked loch, tire of Cathy's teasing,
of her hidden motives,
as I tired of trying to recover your name?
"Don't torture me," he cried to her as she lay dying.

"Don't torture me," I whisper to words
that dissolve into mist as I reach for them.
Simpler in spirit and mind than Heathcliff,
I end my torment, turn to a woman
whose memory is greener than mine,
and try not to wince as she effortlessly
remembers your name.

Jim Crow Crayons

How
arrogant
to name
a crayon: FLESH.
Whose? Not mine or yours.
The color, a blur of pink and peach,
draws an American fiction, a land where light-
    skinned kids fill every playground.

                    No
                  playmates
              speaking Spanish
          answering to names
        not found in the books
    about Dick and Jane. No friends from families
  with slavery in their history, whose stories for
      children explore *shtetls* or mosques.

One
shade,
one choice.
Scope so slim
but so wide in hubris.
The box denies all birthrights beyond Europe's borders,
its mix of colors segregated until the muscle of history
    opens the lid.

An Angel Flowers

Task for the golem*: Fulfill a child's wish.

Abbey needed help.
Her nightly dreams about angels
convinced her one could make her well.
Maybe forever, maybe for just a while.

She shouted at the springtime sky,
hoped an angel would hear.
Instead she conjured a golem.
He couldn't cure Abbey
so he decided to bring her an angel.

The golem created a kaleidoscope
of flowers in a park where the child often rested.
He persuaded the wind to twirl,
bend, loop, weave through the blooms,
freeing petals to play in the air, form shapes.

Apple Blossoms fabricated fluttering wings.
Crocus and Hyacinth designed
a diaphanous robe that danced
around a lithe body of stems and leaves.
A rainbow of Tulips molded a face
with a mesmerizing smile, tender eyes.

The golem's angel found Abbey
sitting on a bench and enveloped

the little girl in her velvety wings,

healing, consoling, loving her.

As he sank into the arms of soil nearby,

the golem knew Abbey's memories

of this angel would be a balm,

ease symptoms, effects, treatments.

Maybe forever, maybe for just a while.

*A golem is a mud and dirt creature in Jewish folklore summoned from the earth to accomplish a task dictated by its creator. Then it returns to the earth, becoming mud and dirt again.

Linda Rodriguez

Linda Rodriguez has published 12 books. Her co-edited anthology, *Unpapered: Writers Consider Native American Identity* and *Cultural Belonging*, will publish in 2023. Her novels—*Every Hidden Fear, Every Broken Trust, Every Last Secret*—and books of poetry— *Dark Sister, Heart's Migration, and Skin Hunger*—have received critical recognition and awards, such as St. Martin's Press/Malice Domestic Best First Novel, International Latino Book Award, Thorpe Menn Award for Literary Excellence, Latina Book Club Best Book, Midwest Voices & Visions, and Ragdale and Macondo fellowships. Rodriguez is past chair of AWP Indigenous Writer's Caucus, founding board member of Latino Writers Collective and The Writers Place, and member of Native Writers Circle of the Americas, Wordcraft Circle of Native American Writers and Storytellers, and Kansas City Cherokee Community.http://lindarodriguezwrites.blogspot.com.

The Wild City

Sprawling across the Kansas and Missouri
River confluence, network of tributaries
woven around bluffs and glaciated hills,
crow-blue in the distance but green, green
as the hearts of trees in the walking,
even today, Kansas City has still-wild parks,
large, well-treed lots, and wooded streams,
homes for foxes, wild turkey, deer, coyote,
interrupting traffic patterns with flight
paths of herons, hawks, and eagles,
a metropolis of small towns linked
by the scent of water and new growth.

Smaller rivers fill out the web
of water that holds the landscape
together, leaf veins feeding surfaces
of green—Blue River, Platte River,
Little Blue River, Little Platte River,
Marais des Cygnes River.
Creeks like Indian Creek, Brush Creek,
Line Creek, First Creek, Second Creek,
Shoal Creek, Willow Creek,
Mill Creek fan out, capillaries
for the breathing system that is the city.

Once, driving along the Little Blue,
I startled at the sudden appearance,

slow flap of huge white wings
banded with black, bright red cap
leading the way ahead of stretched-out
snake neck, legs trailing behind, a legend
rising next to me and taking flight,
whooping crane on migration,
resting and feeding a day or two
in the heart of the city.

When we humans go at last,
by bomb, virus, famine,
disaster, natural or otherwise,
the wild will reclaim Kansas City
in short order, never having completely
released its original hold.

DREAMING OF MY LATE MOTHER-IN-LAW'S HOUSE

Smelling the sharp incense,
cumin and jalapeños,
I cross her floors
again, gold and white shag leading
past couch-flowers.
The television, an altar, always holds
fourteen family faces,
purple candles and Our Lady
of Guadalupe.

In the dining room,
Christ, crucified,
oversees holiday feasts,
and the corner between two doorways
holds the celebrant's chair
with gilded legs. Her sight
stolen by diabetes, Jennie
swivels—never rocks—from voice to voice,
answering with a high laugh like a child's
in an empty choirloft,
offering counsel and comfort
with a flutter of dove-plump hands.

Thermostats set at eighty
make sleep slow to come
in her high beds
while dried palm fronds, blessed

on Passion Sunday,
rattle against the lintels
and hold our city souls
inviolate
in that sacramental house
sanctified by holy water and her.

No More (Sestina For Standing Rock)

I have run out of time
and patience with news coverage so
lazy and biased with a bow
always to
the company owners, powerful and rich,
and to what they want said.

It never matters what my people have said
again and again. Every time
government or corporate forces, so
violent and powerful, require us to bow
in submission, and we won't, the rich
dictate what's broadcast—and written, too.

When I try to explain to
well-meaning white friends, they've said,
"But disorder!" to which I reply each time,
"But oppression!" and sow
seeds of doubt in their comfort. The bough
must break some time and dump the rich

into the mud with the rest of us. The rich
tapestry of cultures that we are can't be reduced to
only WASP—Native, Black, Latino said
to be lesser, negligible, inferior. Each time
I hear this, the fire of anger grows within, so
hot and fierce. It's time for the ruling class's farewell bow.

So long we've stayed peaceful. Soon, it may be time for bow
and lance and rifle, if the rich
can't be compelled to lift the boot, too
sure of their own power to listen to what we've said.
They don't realize it, but they're running out of time.
In arrogance, they rip the fabric of the nation we sew

back together in new, shiny shapes, so
colorful, strange, stronger, tied with the bright bow
of human dignity and rich
gleam of equality and justice. To
those who've always had power and said
to the rest of us, "Give us time
to dole out bits of freedom," we say, "No," so...

You've run out of time. Now, reap what you sow.
We'll no longer bow in submission to
the demands of the white and rich. Hear what we've said.

What River Says

The Cherokee call me Long Man,
yun wi gun hi ta,
because my body stretches and unravels
with my head in the mountains
and my feet resting in the ocean.
I constantly speak words of wisdom
to those who can understand me—
fewer every day.
It takes a quality of attention
fit for magicians or poets.
I have much to tell those
who expend the time and energy to listen.
I have seen so many things.
I know the history of rain
intimately, leaning on the world
to feel it on my skin
and take it inside me
to swell my body. Maybe,
they should have called me Long Woman.

I remember when
the mountains were home only to gods.
I knew your ancestors,
now tangled in the ground.
I swallowed my share and more.
I have seen innumerable generations
living into their deaths.

I am acquainted with the bones of earth,
ancient as the word of God
and stronger by far.
Men have tried forever
to change me and chain me,
but I still wander where I will
when I grow tired of being tame.
I remain the promise of tomorrow,
the hope of new growth
that haunts the night with hypnotic murmurs
and softens the edge between act and dream.

When all hope has fled,
come to me.

Crow Mother (for Frida Kahlo)

They have a memory for faces, my pretty birds.
They are believers in vengeance.
Forgiveness is not in their DNA.
My shiny black sweethearts
will eat out the hearts of those who harm them
one day.

This is why I love them so.
They are like me
in their smart fierceness,
their desire for payback.
We who have been hurt
part our shiny black hair
down the middle,
tuck in a flower or two,
pull on layers of bright fabric
for camouflage,
and sharpen our talons and beaks
in anticipation.

I will curve my claws into paintbrushes
and carve my revenge into the souls
of those who wrong me.
I abstain from forgiveness
of grave accidents. Neither Diego nor God
shall escape me.
This is why I live on
when they are dead.

We recognize the human in the crow
and the caw at the base
of every human throat.

Come, my black beauties!
I've lost my wings, but you
can stab me with your beaks,
hundreds of you,
and hold me in the air
above life's afflictions.
Don't fear the pain you'll inflict.
It won't be the first time I've suffered
the death of *unos quantos piquetitos.*

I hadn't planned on living eternally
in that cursed America, alive
on every bottle and tchotchke,
photoshopped onto muscular bodies
in jockey shorts, the U.S.'s favorite saleswoman.
But no one knows who Diego is any longer,
except as the bastard who drove me mad.
Pierce me, my sweet little carrion eaters,
and lift me into eternal life in a cloud of bloody revenge.

The Things She Gave Me

For Juana (Jenny) Gomez Rodriguez

I remember the faces of my children on summer evenings
when their abuela cried, "Don't leave this yard, *niñitos,*
or *La Llorona* will get you!"
Eyes huge with horror, they stared into the twilight
like two featherless owls, those harbingers of death.

¡Ay! La Llorona, the woman in white,
wandering the night in tears for the children she drowned,
looking for new little victims.
Everyone in the family had encountered her ghostly figure
or heard her wails one night or another.
More than once, I'd glimpsed her
vanishing from the corner of my sight.

Who was more terrified of such a murderous mother,
my little daughter and son or me, too young,
loving them so, but struggling to find or make a self
among the twisted cords of demands?

My own mother shared common ground with *La Llorona,*
for neglect and coldness are a kind of death
to the heart of any child. Could this struggle turn me
into ice against my own little ones?
Like them, I turned my eyes to Jenny,
born Juana in Jalisco,
mother to more than their father and *tios.*

When I married her youngest, we found each other,
the woman with only sons and the girl with no real mother.
She called me *hija*, taught me things she'd longed to teach
a daughter, the secrets of making killer enchiladas
and *pozole*, how to comfort child or man
without weakening either,
how to pray the rosary and make a novena.

With Jenny as model, how could I fear the night
and *La Llorona's* wailing? She showed me how to live
so that those cords couldn't cut yet never broke.

Still, I came to understand grief that sent you
roaming the nights forever when Jenny finally slipped away,
leaving such a hole in the world
that surely none could survive. We did,
as we have a habit of doing, but she remains with me,
after all, in the things she gave me.

The pewter plate engraved with Our Lady of Guadalupe
on my kitchen wall, the cast-iron *placa*
on which I make tortillas (or used to),
the big lavastone *metate* her mother carried
crossing the border, along with the cutting
of night-blooming cereus whose descendants thrive
in my windowsill garden. Jenny lives on in the heart
she taught me to use instead of protecting.

I live another life now, but on rare summer nights
I can hear the sounds of weeping in the darkness
or see a wisp of white at the side of my vision
while I'm walking the dog who stiffens and growls
at nothing. *La Llorona*, go in peace. After all,
the only thing that separates us
is that best of women
and all the things she gave me.

Ofrenda

This is the altar I'm building
to my *calaverada*,
that madcap dance of death
my heart tangoed with you.
Boxes stacked and covered with fabric
to make a place of power
to draw you back to me.
A *calavera* of great artistry
will stand in for you, mimicking life
almost as well as you mimicked love.
I will bake you *pan de muerto* and *rosquete*,
still trying to please you,
buy finest bourbon, your favorite,
no *mezcal* or *tequila* for you,
place it next to the water, salt, and bread.
Mustn't forget the mirror and comb
so you can check your hair
of which you were always so vain.
I will slice my fingers cutting
papel picado skulls and hearts,
yellow, orange, pink and white,
and purple for pain,
to decorate the velvet of the altar.

I adorn the ofrenda and myself
with bright, guilt-swallowing marigolds,
chaining them through my hair,

string their petals across the ground
to lead you back. Let me light the *copal*
and inhale the sweet smoke,
trying to attract you even now,
drawing you to me. Mustn't cry, though.
"The path back to the living world
must not be made slippery by tears."
It will all be to no avail.
I can't fool you or anyone
into thinking I have finally found acceptance.
It's all too clear I would wrestle
the Lady of the Dead herself
for possession, to wrench you
from peaceful rest in Mictlan
and back into the tempest
that was us.

Outside Your House At Midnight, Coyote

stands in shadows, only the red eye
of his cigarette showing his presence.
He watches lights in windows
downstairs and your silhouette
against curtains as you move
from room to room, readying for bed.
He grinds cigarette into the ground
with his boot, to join the others
littering the spot where he lurks,
across the street, vacant lot,
under trees along the fence line.

As you switch off lights,
room by room, and climb stairs
to your bed, Coyote moves out
of the shadows, closer to you
by a few feet more. The outer rays
of the light on the corner
catch his sharp features, golden hair,
the hunger on his face.

He watches your light click on upstairs.
Closing his eyes, Coyote can see within
your walls as you undress and slide under
covers. Tendons in his neck stand out,
rigid with tension, and he swallows his own
wanting with pain. He opens his eyes

to the dark again, watches your last light
wink out, whispers something so soft
even he won't hear, stays to witness
the vulnerability of your restless body.

Sleep. Coyote's standing watch.

Reading At Night

In the dead night's silence
the cards whisper
in my hands.
sliding against and between
each other, rip and riffle,
keeping me company.
I spread them on my bed,
making a pattern
old as Morgan and Merlin.
The Lovers crossed
by The Tower, choose
and the walls come tumbling
across my tufted quilt,
the final outcome
The Hanged Man.
I sit with my back to the dark,
seeking some portent,
any sign of you,
shuffling the future
in my hands.

Conversation With My Mother's Picture

You and Dad were entirely happy here—
you in purple miniskirt, white vest and tights
(you always wore what was already too young
for me), Dad in purple striped pants,
a Kansas State newsboy's cap
made for a bigger man's head.
You both held Wildcat flags and megaphones
to cheer the football team who,
like the rest of the college, despised you
middle-aged townies, arranging for their penicillin
and pregnancy tests and selling them
cameras and stereos at deep discount.
But you were happy
in this picture, before they found
oat-cells in your lungs.

After the verdict, he took you to Disneyland,
this man who married you and your five children
when I was fifteen. He took you cross-country
to visit your family, unseen
since your messy divorce.
He took you to St. Louis
and Six Flags Over Texas and to Topeka
for radiation treatments.
I don't think he ever believed
you could die. Now he's going
the same way. And none of us

live in that Wildcat town with the man
who earned his "Dad" the hard way
from suspicious kids and nursed
your last days. For me, this new dying
brings back yours, leaving me only this image
of you both cheering for lucky winners.

Jemshed Khan

J. Khan is based in the midwestern US and has published in diverse magazines including *Coal City Review, Chiron, SPRR, I-70 Review, Rigorous, Unlikely Stories, Fifth Estate, Writers Resist, Barzakh, and shufPoetry*. In 2021 his activist chapbook *Speech in an Age of Certainty* was released by Finishing Line Press. He is completing a full-length book that narrates the underworld adventures of the Maya Hero Twins as an illustrated epic poem.

Jesús de Honduras, 2020

In Copán Ruinas,
Jesús leads me
to a downtown dealer
with a stash of jade beads
dug by night
from a burial chamber
beneath a stair-stepped pyramid.
The man is slow to smile,
closes the shutters
and throws a wary glance.

When I need a motorcycle,
Jesús finds three.
Their tanks are near empty.
No helmets.
The Kawasaki fits my height.
I fill up at the Puma station
and touch my beads for luck
before heading up gravel roads
twisting into Ch'orti' hill country.

On a rutted hairpin turn
I remember Jesús warning,
Amigo, one bad spill and you're dead.
Who can put blood back in the marrow?
I consider, no hospital or neurosurgeon
for 200 miles, but the wind

is in my gringo hair,
the jungle flying beside,
and I am on the throttle.
I break the back wheel loose
and lean into the wicked curve.

Slowly They Go

I expected handcuff clicks about the wrists,
eyes red with pepper spray, a haze of tear gas,
cell phone videos capturing troubled days.

Too late I realized the cunning gist
of protests that shimmer on-screen.
Slowly scenes disappear from the net,

first the Neo Nazi's, then the homeless Vets.
Facebook and Google delete the rest.
No bullet, no blindfold, no cigarette.

The Tame Swans of Waterbury

Passion or conquest, wander where they will,
attend upon them still

-WB Yeats

The small waterway surrounds an island where swans
sleep on open ground. Each neck and head turned back
and resting along the groove of back and wing.

                Their feathers were trimmed back
in swanling time. They will never fly, but nest and court
and mate by the seasonal clock. It is March. They dunk
their heads and necks in a floating dance. He flat-foots himself
onto her broad back and lifts her neck with his beak
as she sinks.

                                After that awkwardness,
they nuzzle as if posing for calendar shots. For weeks they bicker
over branches and twigs as they build a five-foot-wide nest
with foot-thick walls where she lays her clutch.

        The apartment manager notices, dons her hip waders,
crosses the ornamental stream and rushes the nest. The hissing
cob rises up and beats back with the tough carpal bones of his
wings, but she carries a shield. We hear clamoring wings,
knocking bones and watch from apartment deck as she switches
out the pale clutch, leaves wooden eggs. Commotion subsides.
The thief retreats and the pair returns to tending hatchling
dreams.

The Colonised Mind

*What any colonial system does: impose its tongue
on the subject races.*

—Ngugi wa Thiong'o, "Decolonising the Mind"

For me, it is already done:
My parents' ghazals shushed and mute;
their language siphoned away
by force of nursery rhyme, church choirs,
by various baptismal schemes.

Colonial garrisons occupy
the language centers of my brain—
my thinking circuits click the Anglo way.
Something was traded for wampum,
Venetian beads, cowrie shells...
my tongue twists but cannot say.

DNA still drives my bones and skin
but I am tongue-tied, beset historically.
Far from nest or clan or den,
my diaspora brain adapts as best it can—
colonised because language can.

Interrogator

When you break me,
and I say this because
I have always felt breakable,
consult your field manual
designed for such situations
by committees of paid ethicists,
jailers, and Psychologists
and dumbed to a sixth-grade level
by an otherwise decent
Ivy League MFA graduate.

Pain, hypoxia, ice, fire, or threat
should do the job. Dunk me underwater
and I will not be stoic.
I know my lungs' inward scream,
my brain's struggle with terror
when drowning
for a minute and twenty seconds.

Because suddenly this confession
has come down to my want for air
& I will confess anything you ask
including statements swearing
I was not coerced.
No need to make this difficult.
Look, your superiors already applaud
your work with satisfaction.
Now, where does one sign?

UK Winter, 1963

Page and monarch, forth they went, forth they went together
through the rude wind's bitter lament and the bitter weather.

—John Mason Neale, 1853

I set out to school
in a flimsy anorak,

sleet nips,
teeth click in arctic chill.

My breath frosts the invisible,
I tongue-taste snow.

Goose bumps sting.
Feet skirt puddle mix

but slush seeps the insoles,
and toes turn cold.

My socks squish each step
until inside school.

Teacher prays,
Let us hymn the day

Good King Wenceslas looked out,
on the Feast of Steven,
When the snow lay round about,
deep and crisp and even.

Outside the window,
large flakes tumble.

By break time
I am warm, I am King,

white velvets everything.

Wingnuts

Dad complains that his Makita drill
got lost in the move from the suburbs

to the ground floor apartment
around the corner from my place.

He doesn't know I gave it to Mike
who shoveled Dad's sloped driveway

for umpteen rustbelt winters
because no one on the cul-de-sac

wants to see my old man crack a hip
shuffling back from the mailbox

with a large print Reader's Digest
and a stack of AARP offers.

I drive Dad to Lowe's
where he picks out a cordless Ryobi drill.

In checkout he reaches into his wallet,
tries to pay with his Medicare card.

Queued behind us: Craig's List fix-it guys.
They roll their eyes and scatter to a faster lane.

I'm in no hurry. I like the way the cashier
looks up to me with her quizzical half smile,

as if Dad could be her *abuelito.*
I announce to everyone in earshot

that I have my senior under control:
Dad, I say, *I have your credit card.*

I wink, swipe it once and fake
his shaky scrawl.

Dad's Last ER Visit

Cortical atrophy, says the ER doc
meaning atoms and molecules

are missing

seasons, skies,
constellations are cratering
as his brain retreats
like a galaxy
into its own black hole
like a child into fitful sleep.

I watch

as each thought   gasps
and flops   like a fish
out of water   he mouths
the silent air   not for air
but for   words

Move closer, stray light flickers
in his eyes. Lips move towards a name
he called you when you were young
and the night sky shone bright
in a forever kind of way.
That was long ago.
That was then
& far away.

First Ladies Speak

Jackie-O: You must continue.
                             Poets are the ones
                             who change the world.

Lady Bird: I've really tried to learn the art
                             of clothes, because you don't sell
                             for what you're worth unless you
                             look good.

The Nixon Years: You can't underestimate the
                             power of fear.

                             I have sacrificed everything
                             that I consider precious to advance
                             the career of my husband.

Betty F: Being a lady does not require silence.

Rosalynn: People with mental problems
                             are our neighbors.

Nancy: I think more
                             people would be alive today
                             if there were a death penalty.

                             For eight years, I was sleeping with
                             the president, and if that doesn't give

you special access,
I don't know what does!

Barbara Bush: I married the first man
                   I ever kissed. When I tell this to my
                   children, they just about throw up.

Laura B:

HRC: Hillary Clinton at the end of the day
                   will be a friend of Wall Street.

I say a lot of things — millions of words a day — so if I
misspoke, that was just a misstatement.

Michelle O: I hate diversity
                   workshops. Real change comes
                   from having enough comfort
                   to be really honest and say something
                   very uncomfortable.

I have never been proud of America
my entire adult life.

Melania: If he would only listen.

Maryville High School, 1973

Raymond Gunn: a 27-year-old African American man torched
by a white mob in Maryville, Missouri, USA, January 12, 1931.

--Wikipedia.com

Our neighbor Stokes spits across the fence,
calls us *A-rabs with dirty petrodollars.*
I don't say anything
because a half mile north of here, back in '31,
townsfolk with rope and gasoline,
marched Raymond Gunn to the schoolhouse.
A man wearing a red coat set the fire—
locally known, never named, never tried.

In school most kids leave me alone.
I avoid Ronny Hecker who badgers me
in sing-song gibberish
while his circling friends smile and smirk.

What scares me is trouble from the Smith boys:
brothers who locked a piglet with the runs
in Joe Lempert's gymnasium locker.
For Show-and-Tell they bring a Mason jar
with Raymond's dark finger: severed, charred.

At our ten-year high school reunion,
Ron buys me a beer at the Dew Drop Inn.
I'm sorry, he says, *I learned racism*

at home from dad. We shake hands, bear hug.
I crook an arm across his shoulder: Ron,
you never creeped me out like them Smith boys.

We brag about our high school pranks, the girls
we knew, the cars wrecked. About the Smiths,
Ron says, They're doing life for murder one.

Poet T.L. Sanders

Poet T.L. Sanders is a writer, performer, and career educator who embraces the value of our shared stories. He is a former elementary, middle, and high school English teacher, and current Director of Friends of Frontier Mentoring program. His book, *kNew: Poetic Screenplay*–published by Flying Ketchup Press, became a solo show. The show inspired an arthouse film called, *The kNew-Born*. Whether he is speaking, teaching, writing, or breathing, Poet has a passion for empowering people.

Forest Green

It's beauty
The moonlit night highlights the path critters took
From forests foraging for food to find something good
To give–first
Then wait–a second
For, as they say, the third time is a charm
A charm that thaws needs should love freeze
It's beauty
Giving one chills
The kind one feels surrounded
By the muted sounds of a snow-filled town
Where a son sits unsettled on a wet coat
Post a sunset settled on the west coast
It's beauty
Gives one chills the kind one feels surrounded
By nothing because everything is unsheltered
Usually,
Beauty is a daughter
Today's it lies in the eye of the honest beholder
Who hopes his soul gets what his spirit lacks
He holds an old hat half-filled with lent
and pocket change from passersby
As time passes by He feels a half-
empty longing to be
To be filled with borrowed love
for a change or chance or a shot
Not like a hot toddy

More like an opportunity

To give—first

Then wait—a second

For, as they say, the third time is a charm

And its beauty

An Interview for Tomorrow

Is the future
Promised
Or broken promises
Or promises broken and fixed and broken again

Is the future
Black
Or white
Or mixed with hints of hue

Is the future
Old
Or new
Or aged like the bubbling of icebergs

Is the future
A place
Or a person
Or a state of mind?

Is the future
A way,
Or a street
Or a path picked en route to our now?

Is the future a noun
Or a verb

Or a part of speech
We speak when sharing dreams of tomorrow?

Is the future
Our future
Or our past
Or our present, a gift meant to last
for less than a second

Is the future
Alive arriving
On the wings
Of a phoenix rising like the sun

Is it nascent enough
for one to touch
To hold on to
To carry it like a may be

Maybe the future is a mama tree
Mourning the birth of her baby
For she knows her little future will leave
before it can see the fruits of its seed

Is the future what one likes to think about
But hates to live
Or more like
What one hates to think about
But loves to live

Is the future a solid
Or a liquid
Or a gas
Or plasma
Does the future matter?

No matter,
The future is
The future can
The future will
The future must

Just like us

Light Cones

The Godhead feels

It is inevitable that WE centrifugal-force the
multivariable calculus and linear
algebra behind the theory of Einstein's
Relativity similar to algorithms repeating the future
existence of new frames preceding names of deities—
man-made

The Godheart thinks

What? NO!
Let US let this
Generation generate its own light cones

What if they potter their way
to create more verbs than nouns
then add toes to tow their fate
to make light feet from the ground up to the sky

What if they ground up clay soil
then water it with peace
instead of colloquial beef—
it's the fortunate future they meet

What if they close eyes to watch and to see
the fall of winter and the rise of spring
the malleable magic tomorrow's May brings
to feel the aftermath of April's rain

and welcome the flood of emotions
summer's solstice may be someone's solace

Let us let this
Generation notice

Notice when skin knows no breeze and faith is forced
to feel Fate's lush, green forest and jutting cliffs at the
lips of friendly peaks and mountain streams that lead
to shimmering lake sounds / Notice how the sun-soaked
slopes cloak the life Night brings / Notice why ears
breathe in the underfoot shoosh of satisfied sand / Notice
the waning moon for whom harbingers await wanting
to witness glimmers of rumination / Notice what lost
treasures peer out from the shadows of a torn veil

Let us let this
Generation know that

Then

When they seek shall be what they *see*. When
they see shall be what they *seed*. *When* they
seed shall be what they *grow*. When they grow
shall be what they *know*. When they know… they *shall
be the reap* of fruit from seeds to see
nascent change

Just to be…
born again

to breath again
to be
bold enough to dream

Again to know what feelings feel like
Again to love
Again to like
Again to both let go and hold the might
And then maybe they might have a future

For Love

If not for love
Then for what?

For love fills up empty cups
Love holds old Soul

The Lull
The Like
The Lust

For love to live
then love must love

If not for love
Then for what?

To My Dear Neighbor,

Do you notice
When we are
On our neighborhood trail
Our neighborhood badges
Badger me with questions?
Agitating the adage: "You don't belong here."

Agitated, I dodge the volunteer brigadier
Who would not hear my, "I belong"
Song sang like the Broadway "Rent" I paid
To walk along the walkway under six feet away
From my freshly paved, blacktop driveway

Dear Neighbor,
Do you notice how
The badgeless beard
Benjamin 'Benny' Coffin number III
Barricades, me, your neighbor–an affront
In front of my own garage?

Neighbor,
Tell them you noticed
The berating barrage
Of expletives
Tell them how
I exited
This bloody mess

Triggered a loud love for the hate
His soul was holding exploded my skull
Knees buckled; He's belting
Bare-knuckled bullets through my brain
Though my body barely breathes

Neighbor,
Tell them you see the fire-
Arm of his luger Heimlich maneuver
My chest pressed and soaked, throat choked,
By Beretta smoke laced with bitter Skittles' taste
The rainbow of unalienable rights like Life,
Liberty and the Pursuit of Happiness denied
Sentenced to death for attempted comply

Dear Neighbor,
At least, please capture this chapter
Let your camera phone answer the question
Then leave a message that these unchaperoned
Chaperones have haphazard reactions to mishaps
And happenstance keeps hap-hap-hap-hap-
Happening to hapless hopefuls' family members
Forever remembering crime scene photos
3 March - 7:30 PM

Neighbor, show them how I told the truth
And still, I lie
Drowning in my pool of blood
Adjacent to my pool behind
My house will be paid off from the life
Insurance check my wife collects

Neighbor,

Will you pay your respects?

I need you to notice!

Tell them you know this man
Is your neighbor
Tell then now
Not later

      Neighbor!
          Will you notice?

Alinea

Are we the dream; the wings; the key?

Are we the trompe l'œil believed, ou
sommes-nous the words for "flip the bird"
or the song's dopamine
being the body
language seen dans ballet?

Oui et Nope!
We are the hope

Inspiring the awe-
-some opportunities
to own the open space
to rise over all
obstacles hanging in our way

And si we wings
decide to fly
defy the heights of the high
What's next?

We *soutenons ce rêve*

Et continuons avec le vent
Even when we won't
Understand what fate is saying

Continuons avec la confiance de l'air tsunami
Il nous poussera
Oui…

Le même vent sous les ailes des anges nous poussera
En même temps
Communiquerons la mission
"¡Carpe diem quam minimum credula postero!"
Without question

Sans question, there are *quelqu'un* who
Paints *pour peindre*
Writes *pour écrire*
Sings *pour chanter*
Dances *pour danser*
And that… is okay—*C'est ordinaire*
But she
is Not a painter
And he
is Not a writer
Nor they a singer
So we are Not a dancer
Mais oui
We birds of a feather
add layers and flavors of
les bisous colorés
épanouis et doux;

Don't you understand?
C'est les mots and les movements

The universal language mixed with a hint of
quodlibet et aussi bien déjà vu
The feeling is familiar... familier
Hence, since we are not merely a listener
we are not limited to one sense
And since nous ne sommes pas a painter,
we are not limited to one color
Et puisque nous ne sommes pas a writer,
nous ne sommes pas limités to one word
Et puisque nous ne sommes pas un chanteur,
nous ne sommes pas limités to one song
Et puisque we are not a key,
we are not limited to one door

For it is not through doors
We enter
Through eyes and minds and lives–Our own
To realize the Innate

Oui–With this truth we awake

Et maintenant,
nous nous permettons d'entrer

Since we are not asleep, we are limited to one dream

Truth

A hollow cave deep within
its feelings hinge in time

It's time
to reach for humble hope,
a noble rope that binds boundless vines

A hallowed cry—a swear by life's divine
to search and weep and seek to be
the try that never finds

A nevermind
can cave the chest
of us all and cause the called to call the quits

This nevermind collapses fallen tears that drip
atop the treasured chest that hides
within a hollow cave
just behind a second time

In Time

Fear leads life
Life dreads death
Death seeks truth in Time

No matter the year, the season, the month or moment
Most fears are distant whispers
screaming reasons life is to be absent light

A heaviness
A scared to death - Time ticks till one's breath slips away
No care for race or age or sex
Some say it's wrong but Time is right.

Yeah, Time is always right on time
So, is it time?

Fear, life, death, seek, truth, it is time

Remodeled

My home
Is the only place I've ever known
Hometown Indianapolis
But that town is not
Ironically, my home isn't a house built from earth
Though its canvas is a clean brown like dirt

My country
Tis of thee
Sweet land of liberty
Where I can say
My home is not a house
My home is not a place
My home is not a country
Not a town
Is not a city, but a state
Of being

My being
And this state is being remodeled
Constantly
Getting stronger the longer I live
Even when visiting architects create wreck rooms
To parts of me that have no room to add to

We Cover the Cover

We've read the works the GREATS created
And lived and loved and died and hated
Our lives' reflection—frustrated, relieved
Because in the characters ourselves we see

Now, let's believe it's meant to be
We cover the cover of our story
We write it down from head to tail
We tell our tales both bad and well

We author books, our former dreams
From which we wake and paint the themes
A phrase, one word to three—four
More pages enslaved 'til we release
Ourselves we see penned deep in color

For it's our names written on the covers

Victoria Garton

Victoria Garton began writing poetry in 1976 while studying with Dave Smith, poet. She has published since 1978 in journals such as *Prairie Schooner, Cimarron Review, Quarterly West, Poem, The Sow's Ear Poetry Review, Gasconade Review, River City Poetry, I-70 Review,* and *Thorny Locust.* Her books are *Pout of Tangerine Tango* (Finishing Line Press, 2022) and *Kisses in the Raw Night* (BkMk Press, 1989). She retired from teaching composition and literature at Crowder College in 2020. She has traveled extensively, always observing from her rural Missouri perspective, and currently lives on a cattle ranch with husband Norman.

At the Acropolis

The tourists like fleas hop about
looking not at the Parthenon,
but for a guide to attach to,
suck up information they'll soon forget.

They congregate so densely
at the Temple of Athena Nike,
I must look down to find an occasional
slick stone for walking past.

Finally at the Athena Parthenos
I look for the slight bulges in columns
Iktinos used for perfect symmetry
or its illusion.

I am perfectly foiled by scaffolding
and cranes crooking necks over the structure
and all those others like myself
who want to see more than they can see.

At the Erechtheion, crowds thin and
I marvel at the Caryatids, six stone women
with the roof on their heads.
Forget Atlas holding the world, I am impressed.

Delphic Oracle

She sits in the middle of The Temple of Apollo,
higher than the Sacred Way where pilgrims
wore the stones smooth. Higher than treasuries
of supplicant cities, past grandeur. Myth
has her chewing laurel leaves, I suspect
something stronger, slightly poisonous.
Her prophecies were always ambiguous,
not so different from poetry.

Despite the sun and lack of anything to chew,
we keep ascending until another sprint track
in a stadium at the top—Pythian Games.
Then, it's downhill to another museum.
A good one: Naxian sphinx, the altar
from the temple of Athena Pronaia, and
a cast bronze charioteer, his face set on
pursuit, a few pieces of his chariot nearby.

I'm sorry to miss the huge golden vase,
but it was carried off in 340 BC.
At the time the religious blamed the locals.
Our bus descends through their descendants.
So much gone before us,
so much gone.

Maybe We Should Have Fed Them

Maybe we should have fed them
not just tied on bandanas against
acrid smoke from scrap oak burning,
as we took turns over the 55-gallon drum
where fire reminded us that heat blesses
even the coldest days of winter
and numb hands regained their ability
to hold a needle to draw blood or
a pen to press against a form and carbon copy.

Maybe we should have brought hay
to the rack thin cows instead of exclaiming
over prominent pen bones, countable ribs,
a look beyond hunger on every face
we caught in the headgate in this god-forsaken
stretch of woods where they'd foraged
for anything chewable, pen oak, scrub brush,
and dead leaves under old snow.
"We" were the vet, a couple of cowboys, and me.

Maybe we should have foregone food,
shared their hunger instead of taking a break
to eat with the locals and warm our toes
until they ached with pins and needles
and almost felt normal when we returned
to the penned-up cows who had broken out
to eat our records. Nothing remained

but blood tubes shut away in the vet body
and one regurgitated sheet of carbon paper.

Maybe we should never have taken the job
helping some rich man in the city
bill the government for diseased animals
he'd starved. I wiped cow slobber
off the paper, matched tubes to numbers,
withstood the anger as the silent cowboys
brought around the unmatched ones, again
did the work of the morning. Then we did
the new herd in the afternoon.

Maybe we should have just quit.
It was cold all right, and ash swirled out
of the 55-gallon drum as we grew too weary
to feed a fire none had the heart to keep burning.
But, we had mortgages, small mouths to feed,
and the vet said we were part of something big,
the eradication of a disease affecting animals
and humans. We finished the job,
grime clinging to our idealism.

After The Rain of Missiles

It is when her feet hit concrete
of the hanger-like building where
she and the others were sheltered
that she must tell herself again and again
that the carpet laid just last year
is gone along with the comfortable bed.

She lifts herself from the narrow cot.
"Refugee," she tries on the word as she waits
in the line for the toilet. Her mind travels
room to room in the home she left.
Her mind will not accept as permanent
this waiting in line to brush the fur from teeth.

In her mind she's on a camping trip,
will savor the primitive, paint number by
number this new picture of her life.
A miniature she'll call an adventure
because the big picture has so much
blank space filling with explosions of fire.

In the rain of missiles it's hard to remember
gratitude. In the rain of missiles only
the present is present, and under it all
the scream that if she lets loose
will fill this hall and sweep away
the gracious welcome of strangers.

Curly Dock

Name like a hired hand, one who shows up
after the hard work of planting.

Long crimped leaves, edges as delicate as pie crust
spread over the crumbly dirt of the garden.

Fleshy taproot holds its place, pops like a champagne cork,
loses its head to grow another.

Bunches of them, here and there, enduring,
recurring. Perennials, existing for infinite time.

Into the fall their flowers without petals
turn the reddish-brown of old blood.

Cast seeds to the wind. Unlike we humans who sow
and reap and cast weeds aside until we can't.

Meanwhile the cardinal in the lilacs encourages
with "Pretty. Pretty." We try to see it his way.

Scarlet flash even in winter. Always brilliant.
Fresh as newly spilled blood, reminding us

of the future we won't attend but pretend we will.
Curly Dock, up for the next season and the next.

Blackberry Blessing

They grow in the fencerow, more on the neighbor's side
than yours. You pick with the delight of rescuing
a goodness that would be otherwise lost.

At first you eat more than you save,
the late July sweetness makes up for the seeds
grown woody as lack of rain shrivels the fruit.

A Japanese beetle buzzes its metallic coat,
rustles the leaves like a stock car tearing ahead,
makes you swerve into the prickly branches.

You extricate your sleeve, gingerly withdraw
your hand, curse the unavoidable pain that
comes to foragers and dreamers.

You save the red, resistant ones, those going to wine,
and those that tumble forth, all resistance gone.
Even so, some fall to the dirt sowing for another season.

Some out of your reach dry into clusters of seeds.
Your leave those like the dreams you harbored,
could almost taste but didn't. Those are for the birds.

When the thorns catch your flesh and bring blood,
it mixes with fruit painting hands purple. Time to go,
and yet another bunch holds you, and another.

Mid-morning when the sun regains its fierceness
you have enough to make a pie and freeze a few against
winter's diet of one fruitless day after another.

Leaving, may you not fall into blackberry brambles
as Lucifer did, but go ripe and succulent with stained
fingertips, berries and dreams still to pick.

The Black Empire-Waist Coat

I got it when images of Jackie in black and white
faded to a white dot in a small round screen.
The collar was white mink, and no one shamed me
when I wore it to the White Christmas Dance,
though years later after I'd made a headband
from the collar, I was called out on the slopes by a skier
in nylon so bright it turned the snow radioactive.

At the White Christmas Dance Miss Walton
agreed it was too expensive to pile on benches
in the locker room and locked it in her classroom.
My friends gathered round to pet the collar
and talk of Jackie and the young President
whose death would break our hearts worse
than boys who kissed and left for rice paddies.

Mother, dad, and I bought it at Nola Leach,
a store for women who cared what people
at dinner parties said. We dressed in our Sunday best
to shop there and tried to not cringe when peeking
at price tags hung discreetly inside the garments.
The owner looked down her nose at us, even
when daddy peeled out the hard-earned $100.00 bill.

Why they decided to spend that kind of money
I still don't know. I sewed most of my dresses.
Perhaps they wanted me to feel valued beyond

what some local farm boy could ever offer?
Perhaps I begged shamelessly? Perhaps mother
wanted more for me than she'd ever had?
Her old coat would do another year, she said.

I'd never had a coat wrapped in white tissue
and entombed in a box with gold letters
that would hold my dried corsages into
the next decade. I'd never had a coat whose
satin lining could have decorated a casket.
I'd never had a coat whose tight twill wool forgave
every touch of fingers buttoning and unbuttoning.

Jackie wore her empire-waist coat to hide
John-John and I wore mine at the university
to hide my unexpected baby bump. Jackie became
Jackie O and didn't need a coat on her Greek Island.
I wore mine again to warm the next baby.
In the psychedelic 70's I wore it with slick leopard
print collar and matching buttons.

When Jackie moved on to a belted trench
and editing books, I hung my empire-waist
in the closet of my childhood room and bought
a belted trench, black of course, and started
sending out my poems. Later, mother brought
the empire-waist out of the closet. Freed the
leopard and wore it with original buttons.

Its roomy Raglan sleeves accommodated
her board shoulders. She wore it off and on
until the millennium. After Jackie died and seven
years later mother, its original box long since
deteriorated and all the corsages crumbled,
I bagged the coat for a vintage shop. It lives
on eBay where Jackie's look is trending.

The Dread the Dream the Stroke

As an airplane roars its intentions to leave this earth
I pray to be forgiven every over-weight ounce of guilt
and I praise every monotonous moment of my life,
a talisman against the dread of falling from the sky.
I always take a window seat to see the clouds
gathering under us to make a trampoline. In dreams
I rise like a hawk, the sun my bullseye, Daedalus
my patron saint, Icarus filling me with false prowess.
The plane shudders, settles itself into routine and
I remind myself these wings are not made of wax.

Grounded I do not fear the dream of Isaac. Abraham
has gathered wood for the sacrifice I do not fear.
As sleep takes me I release a prayer to whatever God
will rule my dreams, but do not fear the knife's pierce,
the blinding fire that enters my skull. They say, "You
will always awake before the final plunge." They lie.
I try to lift my arms like Icarus lifted wings of wax.
I try to walk assured as Isaac trusting a father god.
That's when I know how stealthily harm has come
and fully awake I learn that the dream was real.

Matter of Tense

A down-trodden woman comes and goes from his room.
Everything about her says her hard life just got harder.
He sits shrunken in rehab as a therapist works his shoulder.
His tangle of long hair and beard, trendy in the 70s, white.

His sleeveless shirt with a pouncing eagle says "Freedom"
and that's what all of us in the circle want to regain.
The tattoo of a shield and sword on his right arm flexes
as the muscles move. The left arm droops, flaccid.

Someone has excised layers of skin, rather like reverse
applique to the quilter, to write a single word, "FUCK".
I try not to stare at it, but I stare at it and the English
teacher in me wonders, "Should that be past tense?".

But then everyone here is "fucked" in some way.
My right side is as affected as his left. His left hand
and my right hang unresponsive as dead fish.
Though I can't imagine us paired, I can't help notice

together, we would make a whole functioning person.
We could be ball and chain and will be ball or chain
to those who love us, at least for the foreseeable future.
He's all "What the fuck" attitude as one tells of new knees.

Another a back surgery gone wrong, another like us
has had a stroke. But when we play the memory game
he's all eagerness and longing to match the cute puppies
he never owned in his junkyard dog childhood.

The Comfort of Their Breathing

Unable to descend steps with no rail,
I stood at the door shaking the rug
when from a truck's stalled lights
a solitary light broke off, advanced.
A man's voice cut the silence,
"Cow on the road. Yours?"

In earlier times, I would jump
in the truck, head out, search
until my light pooled in liquid eyes,
bring the lost home, but
I no longer live in earlier times.

With the feeling of helplessness
driven to the bone,
I accept a stranger's help,
call in my kin,
stay housebound with my walker.

Helpers search, but the cow has melted
into darkness. Before sleep comes,
I count the times she clears the electric wire,
walks out the open gate. I wake
from nightmares of her dodging traffic
on the state highway.

At dawn in 9 degrees cold
my husband (returned) heads out
to find her behind an abandoned house,
across the fence from the others.
Though set apart from community,
she has slept in the comfort of their breathing.

Now she walks as if bringing him home,
and I, going window to window,
like a lighthouse track their progress,
an obsolete lighthouse who depends on
a keeper to turn her off as the sun rises
sweeping away the darkness.

Jane Ellen Ibur

Jane Ellen Ibur, Poet Laureate of St Louis, Missouri, is the author of *Both Wings Flappin', Still Not Flyin'* and *The Little Mrs./Misses* both published by PenUltimate Press. She has garnered much recognition as an Arts Educator teaching in underserved communities. She received a Visionary Award for Outstanding Arts Educator; recognized as a Warrior Poet from Word in Motion; two awards from the Missouri Scholar's Academy, A World of Difference Award from the Anti-Defamation League. Honored with an Author Recognition Award by the Missouri Center for the Book. She also received the Loretto Award for Service to Humanity and Social Justice from her alma mater, Webster University. She is published in literary journals and anthologies, receiving additional awards. For further details, visit Ibur's Wikipedia page.

What Mary Said

"Baby, I'd be telling you a lie
if I didn't tell you I had some regrets.
But I have seen ... you don't understand yet.
I really trust the Lord, I put prayers
and faith first. You got to believe in
what you ast for. You might not get it
right now. But you has to have faith.
I can get stirred up so bad until I gets my bible
and I read the 37th Psalm all the way through.
I reads it. You just read it again.
You'll understand what it's telling you to do.
We're all gonna have those kinds of days.
We cain't make it and have no trials or tribulations
at all. I get up in the morning.
I cain't stoop down. I cain't do this
and I cain't do the other, and I sits there
on that bed and I boo hoos, I cries,
water just runs down -
and then I says, 'Well, Lord,
I'm just grateful I can do what I am doing'.
'Cause it's really hard when you used to
could do something and now you cain't do
and you wants to. You got to thank
the Lord for what you have. He didn't promise
you every day it's gonna be sunshine.
'Cause some days it's gonna rain.

Augusta

Your kingdom waning,
I brushed your downy hair
like a lady-in-waiting

I don't remember your voice
or if we spoke at all
when I rummaged through your drawers
past the strands of emeralds and pearls

The brushes and hand mirrors
how royal they were
oval figurines captured forever in motion
as if your youth were entrapped in those brushes
as if I could know your youth
by brushing your hair
as you sat on your rocking chair throne

Your room was a castle
and I traced backwards to find you

You were dead before I knew
learned of your flight from Austria
after your husband deserted to drink
read that your bright son died
after graduation at thirteen
heard that your daughter perished in the great flu
    epidemic

Your three surviving daughters
bartered over who should devote a self to you
in your oldness
until your regime crumbled
and you were imprisoned -
a monarch in exile -
in a hospital cell
awaiting judgment with other inmates,
overgrown children in a permanent nursery,
some tending dolls,
replaying motherhood

You were my first lady
faded queen
I was the handmaiden
for you,
my grandmother's mother
You, once so magnificent
stripped of command, crown,
chaperoned by nurses
remembering nothing

And still you sat
strapped in a rocking chair
quietly waiting for death
to untie you

I inherited your room
the gaping bed swallowed me,
the throne of a rocking chair

where I strained to fit
and expected your return

The rocker, sprayed another color,
sits in my sister's room
with clothes heaped on it

I visit you
bound forever into the ground
with vines
I brush away dead leaves
like hair
wondering how that scrawny, naked
arm of an apple tree
attends you
since my empty hand no longer can

Stagecoach

You remember the bumper pool table
but I see the stagecoach
that carries us from town to town.
Below the basement stairs
cuts that ridge of range
where the trail passes through
the canyon from Laramie
to Virginia City. Driver
roosts on top, while the other
rides shotgun, lookout,
rifle, that favors a pool cue,
cradled in his lap.
We stow the grips topside.
Underneath the table, the coach
a little tight, holds room for four,
alert for renegades or some outlaw
holding up the stage for the miners'
gold tucked in the strongbox
under the driver's seat.
Dust spits everywhere when the horses run.
Bumping along the trail is hell
on a tailbone, 'specially if we hit
a ditch or stone. The road uneven,
irregular, tires out the stock
so we stop over, change horses,
feed and water the spent ones,
maybe rest ourselves overnight,

stretching the legs a spell,
rinsing the face and mouth,
grabbing a meal or shot of rye
before we ride off into the sunset.

Lady Dainty

It pressed on me, time running out, time
for one last chance, one more conversation with my
  mother
and of course I felt it most in my gut
flaring up again since last Tuesday
and I feel like a kid again, that child
who failed, who never became Lady Dainty. Read

my cracked lips, I couldn't do it. Not read,
of course. I read to spend my time
in a happier place where I was a pleasant child,
one who turned out right and pleased Mother.
Weekends were hardest, I was such a tom-boy, but
  by Tuesday
I was calmer, pulled into the crowd, invisible gut

cramping and screaming unseen. Shut up, gut,
I say with Librax and Paragoric. I read
to escape, go deep underground, past Tuesday
holding my breath till the return of summertime
when the living was never easy. I tagged after Mother
to Lady Dainty to get her hair done. A child,

I ran errands, brought Cokes from El and Lee, a child
in waiting. I was skinny, drank soda which rotted my
  tender gut.
All I wanted to do was please my Mother,

but I was not that kid. I continued to read
looking for myself in pages in a book. Time
is not enough to heal the thousand Tuesdays.

I climbed trees knowing I was no Sunday or Monday,
    maybe Tuesday,
more likely Thursday, red and green, fairy child.
It took years for that to sink in, so much time
and all the Fridays and Saturdays straight to my gut,
the place where I'm holding it in, so I read.
How do I build the person house with no foundation
    from Mother?

How do I learn to be my own mother,
every day fine, no slump or slouch on Tuesday,
no statistic that ends up in a book I read.
Behind my eyes I will always be a child
but I need to learn to mother my gut
and be fine fall, winter, spring or summertime.

Chiseled in time the mother/child
enigma haunts me most on Tuesdays, here in my gut.
Read me right, please, next time.

Hibiscus

Mom loved the hibiscus I planted
in ceramic pots around the pool.
Annuals with their shiny wax leaves
flowered like crazy after a slow start.
Explosions of crimson they bloomed
their guts out day after day.
When the flowers finished they rolled
themselves into fists like fat cigars
dropped to the deck.
                    She watered
daily, twice most days, shoving the hose
through the chain links, limping and cursing,
slamming water into the soil with such force
the black dirt dove over the sides fearing
for its life and swam away on the sidewalk.
How she loved those blooms.
How she hated their need.

Cool

I could light my cigarette
holding the lit match way
below the tip and it caught,
some science experiment. I
flipped the stub through the air
with thumb and finger like a
whirlybird. Debbie Lewis said
I looked like a sophisticated slut
when I smoked. I liked the dragon
vapor curling up my nose blowing
smoke rings. Things I used to do –
ride horses, crawl in a creek bed
after fossils, snorkel by the shore
shelling when I couldn't walk,
swim in rough water, climb
mountains, remember, parasail,
swim, cruise, climb trees,
get off the floor, walk up stairs,
stand in the shower, walk down-
stairs, walk - all the things I used to do
once upon a time when I was cool.

Mrs. Noah – Two Weeks Out

(after David Leyner)

Today I decide to inventory. I keep a strict log
of everything, from rations to rashes, believing
sanity comes from organization, routine, ritual,
business as usual, once that's established, which
I did immediately. So much chaos and disorder,
grief and fear reign, I choose chores to sandbag
the tidal waves of emotion, and here we are, two
weeks out, doing pretty well for ourselves, horses,
oxen, hooved beasts working in the mill, bees build
a hive, worms churning soil in the agricultural wing,
goats donating for cheese in the dairy, antlered beasts
in the kitchen for hanging utensils, pots and pans, my
daughters-in-law in managerial positions; that's a first.
Noah sits fat and wet on the deck. Daily, he appears
to be swelling. I never see him eating, but things turn
up missing, like the dodo's, the minotaurs, the harpies,
unicorns, chimeras, nymphs, satyrs, gorgons, cyclopses,
sirens, phoenixes, griffins, dinosaurs and dragons.
Perhaps this accounts for the unbelievable foulness of his
morning breath.

Serenity

Grant me the serenity
John should have awakened in an hour and a half,
but he was deep into it. I can only guess at my own
exhaustion and how anesthesia would have affected
me, sleepless for 6 months, nursing him. The staff
let him sleep, not needing the bed, giving me the break.
I shopped for scrubs on the metal shelves near his bed,
pants with elastic waists pressing on his swollen stomach.
The nurses let me take a few pairs, lightweight in the
summer heat, string tied, thin enough to keep his hot
water bottle companion from blistering his tender skin,
to accept the things
The stent, the plastic one once the permanent metal one
was ruled out, installed in his bile duct. Have I said how
much I hate the color yellow, the color of good piss, that
first stained John's underwear, at least three pairs Sondra
bleached daily, but his grew darker, the color of imported
beer, his skin the color of old newspapers thin enough to
flake, or so I feared as I moved the hairbrush out of his
reach to prevent him scratching his arms, his face the
color of dandelions in spring.
I cannot change
I could neither stop nor postpone his death. It came
unheralded one week after my 25th anniversary with
Sondra, one week before my 49th birthday, his itching
unceasing as he lay immersed in warm oatmeal baths,
Marat Sade, his head pillowed on white terrycloth, the window

open, a fan in the doorway blowing over him,
the shower curtain gathered in the middle shielding
his privates covered with a washcloth, the most private of
men, naked, raw. Here he held court, visitors sitting on a
couch facing him.

the courage to change

His death was no accident, rather orchestrated suicide
planned at least two years prior, his plot by Dad's side
secured, casket hand-made, tongue and grooved pine with
a raised Jewish star that stood sentinel in my garage, his
wedding quilt draped over to shield me. Why did he come
to me? Gift? Punishment?

the things I can

Who am I now? Fifteen years of death and burials
beginning with Mary; then the hundreds of male friends
dead from AIDS, all the people in the Make Today Count
support group, Dad, John, and in the following April,
Nancy and Bob. I have seen too much of death, John's life
bleeding out his left side, right where that pain is located that
kept me awake all night. Doctors say cancer doesn't
hurt. Then why the eye-dropper full of morphine every 15
minutes that caked like a syrupy crust in the corners of his
mouth? Why the constant groaning?

and the wisdom to

Day after day I'd bring in the Ensure. "Chocolate or strawberry?
No, I won't set it down. Drink it now while it's
cold." Worse than Nurse Ratchett, pouring the liquid
calories into the Elixir of Joy we renamed the Elixir of
John. After he scaled the bedrails to get to the bathroom
he no longer needed, catheter, colostomy, adult diapers for

my benefit, I tied bells so that if I dozed
the tinkling would wake me. I played Grateful Dead
CD's, Carlos Nakai, the Mamas and Papas, anything
to break the stillness. I draped a purple scarf over the
light shade by his bed to dim the room at night so I
could see his face, drawn, disappearing.

know the difference

He was my brother, felt like my twin as kids. I tried to
reel him back from the edge, like a sleepwalker, like a
lunatic. One day he sang a little song and I'd never in
my life heard his sweet voice, his sweet breath, his soft
lips. His left hand clutched the rail that last night, a
thin film of sweat on his skin, his breath shallow,
purple around his nails and knees. I rose to mine,
clamped my hand over his, said, "I love you, John,"
and he quit breathing, gripping my heart in his fist.

Shooting Stars

(for my brother, John)

Steamy summer days
wetness hangs in the air.
Still only June and John
swims like crazy reaching
for the stars with every stroke.
Slow down, I tell him.
You'll get there soon
enough. I tread water,
not even tired yet.
Sometimes I float on
my back staring at the night
sky and for the first time
in my life I hate the stars
because I know the next
shooting one will be John.

A Hot Dog Kind Of Girl

At least once a year, I climb
the hill to Willhoft's field,
borrow the bat from the boys
who play there, crack a couple
long ones from our property line
to the street. Just to let them know
this girl's still got the grit.
Just boys played khoury league, while I
played the major league stadiums in my mind.
I won't let them forget me
at the plate with my magic bat,
at the Willhoft's party where I
smashed run after run until
the company looked away embarrassed,
feeling betrayed instead of proud. Their silence
pounds loud in my ears.

I look back to an empty ball field,
dust blowing across the infield,
the worn base paths. I've put
on the pounds, can't round
the bases with the speed I once
boasted. The bat's busted,
the ball's unraveled, the glove
still holds the ghost of a ball.

They wanted me all frilly and fake.
I was a hot dog kind of girl,
slider into bases, rider of winds,
mud-dried jeans. I played
rowdy ball, a crowd all by myself;
Spinner, Spinner, Spinner, they chanted.

Then I sent the ball so high
it never came down, but turned
into a star and stayed in the sky.
See that silver glow higher
than the rest? That's the star
with my name on it, that says
I'm the best.

This project was made possible, in part, by generous support from the Osage Arts Community.

Osage Arts Community provides temporary time, space and support for the creation of new artistic works in a retreat format, serving creative people of all kinds — visual artists, composers, poets, fiction and nonfiction writers. Located on a 152-acre farm in an isolated rural mountainside setting in Central Missouri and bordered by ¾ of a mile of the Gasconade River, OAC provides residencies to those working alone, as well as welcoming collaborative teams, offering living space and workspace in a country environment to emerging and mid-career artists. For more information, visit us at www.osageac.org

Osage Arts Community

www.ingramcontent.com/pod-product-compliance
Lightning Source LLC
Chambersburg PA
CBHW031509120626
46545CB00005B/1804